IN THE NAME OF FREEDOM

Enes Kanter Freedom

THRESHOLD EDITIONS

New York   Amsterdam/Antwerp   London   Toronto
Sydney/Melbourne   New Delhi

Threshold Editions
An Imprint of Simon & Schuster, LLC
1230 Avenue of the Americas
New York, NY 10020

Copyright © 2025 by Enes Freedom

All rights reserved, including the right to reproduce this book or portions thereof in any form whatsoever. For information, address Threshold Editions Subsidiary Rights Department, 1230 Avenue of the Americas, New York, NY 10020.

First Threshold Editions hardcover edition October 2025

THRESHOLD EDITIONS and colophon are trademarks of Simon & Schuster, LLC

For information about special discounts for bulk purchases, please contact Simon & Schuster Special Sales at 1-866-506-1949 or business@simonandschuster.com.

The Simon & Schuster Speakers Bureau can bring authors to your live event. For more information, or to book an event, contact the Simon & Schuster Speakers Bureau at 1-866-248-3049 or visit our website at www.simonspeakers.com.

INTERIOR DESIGN BY KARLA SCHWEER

Manufactured in the United States of America

10 9 8 7 6 5 4 3 2 1

Library of Congress Cataloging-in-Publication Data is available.

ISBN 978-1-6680-7836-5

ISBN 978-1-6680-7838-9 (ebook)

*This book is for all who have sacrificed
what they love for freedom.*

CONTENTS

INTRODUCTION ix

1 THE PROMISE 1

2 THE GREAT ESCAPE 19

3 THE NEW WORLD 31

4 KENTUCKY BLUES 41

5 THE LEAGUE CALLS 55

6 BIRTH OF AN ACTIVIST 73

7 ERDOĞAN'S REVENGE 91

8 STANDING ON PRINCIPLE 109

9 CHALLENGING CHINA 131

10 EXILE 153

11 IN MEMORY OF MUHAMMED FETHULLAH GÜLEN 179

12 FREEDOM'S FUTURE 187

ACKNOWLEDGMENTS 201

NOTES 205

INTRODUCTION

Freedom is not free. It comes at a cost. My story, told here, is the price of freedom—a price that is worth paying.

It is a story born from the pain of being disowned by my home country, shut out from contact with my family for ten years, and banished from playing the game I love in the NBA and elsewhere. It is the story of being detained in Europe, almost kidnapped in a foreign country, being labeled an "international criminal," and having an Interpol arrest warrant issued for me. It is the story of imprisoned and tortured family members, countless death threats, twelve arrest warrants, and living with a $500,000 bounty on my head. It is a story of sacrificing all that was most dear to me. It is a story of facing the rest of my life thinking about what could have been, and what may never be. In short, it is a story of being a most wanted man.

But it is also a story of discovering the most precious things of all. For all I have lost, I have gained even more.

As a kid, all I wanted to be was a basketball player. I lived that dream when I got drafted into the NBA in 2011. But as my homeland of Turkey fell further into the clutches of a dictator, I felt a moral obligation to speak out against injustice everywhere and be a voice for those who have no voice—from Turkey, to China, to everywhere else where liberty has no safe quarter. I realized my life had to be bigger than basketball.

Today, everywhere I go, no matter the race, religion, gender, or other background of the person I meet, I have carried the same message: Freedom is not just a word. It's a way of life. The greatest gift of freedom is the ability to choose—to choose love, peace, kindness, and to uplift others. And as we enjoy our freedoms, let's remember those still fighting for theirs.

There is only one country that could have inspired me to do all this: the United States of America. As a child, I viewed the U.S. as a source of evil. But after meeting her people, sharing in her blessings, and reflecting on her ideals, I realized that I was born to be an American. Thus, this book is also an American immigrant's meditations on all that is exceptional in America: her citizens, her opportunities, and—most of all—the freedom she affords all. America is not perfect, but as a man who has had friends and family deprived of their rights and imprisoned, I know it is the most liberty-loving country in the world and a place we should treasure.

I hope my story will entertain and enlighten you. But more than anything, I hope it inspires you to unite with others to stand up for human rights, justice, democracy, and freedom for all.

Enes Kanter Freedom
Washington, D.C.
October 20, 2024, 9:20 p.m.

IN THE NAME OF FREEDOM

CHAPTER 1

THE PROMISE

Boom. Boom. Boom.

The noise at my door in the middle of the night in Jakarta, Indonesia, wasn't a knock. It was a frantic pound.

I snapped awake from a deep and exhausted sleep and looked at the clock: 2:30 a.m. *What's going on?*

I stumbled out of my bed and made my way to the door. Gazing through the peephole, I saw my manager, Mel (his name has been changed to protect his identity). He looked tense and disheveled—a man who had just been jolted awake himself.

I had barely opened the door when Mel whispered to me, "Come to my room immediately. We need to talk." He kept his voice low so that the security guard posted near my door could not hear.

I trusted Mel with almost everything in my life. We'd known each other for years. He had been my translator in college and was now my partner in charity work. If he said it was serious, I had no doubt.

Moments later we were in his room. He looked me dead in the eye and said quietly, "We need to leave immediately."

"What do you mean we need to leave?"

"I got a call from some friends at the school where we held the basketball camp earlier today. Some guys came there tonight looking to 'talk' to you. We don't know who exactly they were, but this could get really dangerous."

The first possibility was that these visitors were kidnappers looking to take me hostage for ransom, as is known to happen to high-profile figures visiting certain Pacific countries. The second possibility was more concerning: agents of the Indonesian government might be looking for me. If they were, that could only mean one thing—the Turkish government was pressuring Indonesia to detain and extradite me.

I don't like to run from bullies. I dismissed Mel's warning as irrational paranoia and suggested we go back to our rooms to get some sleep. But Mel pleaded with me: "We need to escape—this could get really ugly!" It was one of those decisions that really aren't a decision at all: flee or risk falling into the hands of the Turkish dictator, Recep Tayyip Erdoğan, who had made my life a living hell for years. I was almost certain he was behind this.

"Let's go."

We frantically looked up the very next flight out of town—a 5:30 a.m. departure to Singapore. This might be our only chance out.

At 3:10 a.m. we booked two tickets. But as we prepared to move, we realized we had a major problem: escaping my security detail. I was under the protection of the Indonesian government, local police, and my own security team. I had a traveling army with me, including an armed guard at my hotel room door in the middle of the night. Thankfully, Mel made a phone call to create a diversion that brought the door guard to the lobby. We couldn't trust anyone at this moment—not even the guys hired to protect me.

I quickly began shoving some stuff into my bag in the few moments I had before he came back. I was filled with disappointment as much as panic. This was not the way I wanted my time in Indonesia to end. My visit here was part of a seventeen-country, forty-day trip where I held free basketball clinics for kids all over the world. After six years in the NBA, my passion off the court had become sharing the game I loved as a tool to teach kids of all different backgrounds about our shared humanity. Now my work would have to continue elsewhere.

I emerged from my room, leaving the do-not-disturb sign on the door for good measure. Mel and I darted into a stairwell and hustled down the emergency stairs toward the hotel's back exit. We were leaving almost everything behind—many of our belongings, our friends on the tour, and the fleet of cars that accompanied our huge security detail. The interviews and meetings we had scheduled with Indonesian journalists and politicians the next morning would not be happening. We'd either be in jail—some Indonesian government officials under Erdoğan's influence doing a favor to Turkey—or on the next plane out of the country.

It was May 19, 2017, one day before my twenty-fifth birthday. It wasn't exactly the way I planned to start celebrating.

After exiting the emergency stairs around 3:30 a.m., by a stroke of luck we found a taxi within minutes. We told the driver to step on it to the airport. On the way, Mel took a video that we planned to send to our friends and lawyer in America in case anything happened. Cramped in the back seat, Mel explained, "We were told by our local contacts . . . that the Turkish government asked for their help to reach Enes and they need to talk to him. We don't know what their motive is, we don't know what's going on, but we need to make sure Enes is safe." At least we had tried to get away if we were captured, and had evidence of what had happened.

Never has a short car ride seemed like such an eternity. Thankfully, we made it to the airport and hustled through security, holding our breath the entire time—as a 6'11" guy, I'm pretty easy to pick out of a crowd. At any moment, someone in uniform could tap me on the shoulder and say the dreaded phrase "Come with me, please."

Fortunately, that didn't happen—maybe wearing my hoodie and sunglasses helped. After maneuvering myself through the full-body scanners and acting like everything was normal before the eyes of the stern-faced security guards, we made it onto the plane to Singapore, silently praying that we could make it out of the country. We exhaled only when the plane's wheels lifted off the ground.

Two hours later we landed in Singapore. We called a friend who had helped organize our visit to Indonesia to find out who wanted to "talk" to us. We couldn't believe what we heard from him: "The guys who came looking for you were army and intelligence service officers. They were there to take you away. If you had stayed in the country another five or six hours, you'd be on a plane to Turkey."

We were lucky to have escaped, but we weren't out of the woods yet. We had no idea where to go next. Eventually, we decided on Europe—where I believed I would be safe thanks to the European Union's strong human rights laws. We were also scheduled to visit Romania anyway, for a big international cultural festival with six thousand people. Romania it was.

When we landed in the capital of Bucharest, I waited in the immigration line. These lines are normally a mile long to begin with, but this one felt like an eternity, especially as a handful of fellow travelers gawked at my giant frame. When it was my turn to approach the booth, I handed over my passport to the agent checking documents. She examined it for at least ten minutes, her eyes flickering back and forth from her computer screen to the pages. Other people in line behind me were directed away from the area and toward another booth. I got the message: this could take a while. I grew more and more nervous as the minutes ticked by.

I asked the woman checking my passport, "Is there a problem?"

She told me to wait a moment and entered a back room alone. She returned with police.

"Your passport has been revoked. You can't enter the country. There's an arrest warrant out for you."

Turkey, no doubt.

Two Romanian officers in black pants and white shirts then led me away to a holding area. Thankfully, even though he was not detained, Mel remained by my side to offer as much protection as he could. Our minds were cracking with despair as we tried to imagine how this would end.

Then something remarkable happened.

When one of the officers guarding me went to the bathroom, the other one ran toward me. He gasped and spoke quickly: "I love the NBA, and I've been following your activism. I've got to tell you something."

I said, "Do you want an autograph?"

"Forget about an autograph! You have two hours to leave the country. If you're still here then, they're going to send you back to Turkey. The Romanian government and Turkish government have already started conversations about an extradition deal."

Drowning in anxiety that I might soon be extradited back to a country that wanted me dead, I had no idea what to do.

But I did know that I had friends in the United States. And Americans always stand for freedom. It was one of the greatest lessons I'd learned after more than six years in America—the standard-bearer of liberty around the world, and a country that I am today beyond blessed to call my home. I posted a short video to social media documenting my detention and accusing the president of Turkey, Recep Tayyip Erdoğan, of being the perpetrator behind it all—"he is a bad, bad man and he's a dictator." Within minutes, teammates like Steven Adams and Russell Westbrook texted me: Dude, what's going on? They started getting the hashtag #FreeEnes going on social media. #FreeEnes had originally started as a joke protest slogan among the students at the University of Kentucky when I was ineligible to play NCAA basketball. Now it meant something much more serious, and the world was taking note.

Whenever freedom-loving people are in crisis, they look to one nation as their savior: the United States of America. At this point in my career, I was playing for the Oklahoma City Thunder and had become friends with Senator James Lankford of Oklahoma. He was my first phone call.

"I think Turkey's trying to kidnap me," I blurted out as I explained my plight to him. Without hesitation he answered, "I got you. Let me call some people immediately."

I later learned that Senator Lankford had called the Romanian government. Forty-five minutes later a man in a suit emerged to talk with the Romanian guards. To this day, I still have no idea who he was.

Then he came up to me, standing inches from my face. "Leave all your stuff here."

I looked at him, puzzled. He shoved a piece of paper in my hand.

"Here's your ticket. You're going on this flight. Don't even look back."

I stood there stunned. I didn't even know who this guy was!

"Go!"

"What about my luggage?"

My new mystery friend couldn't believe what he was hearing. "You're worrying about luggage right now? Get on the plane!"

I looked at the ticket—it was to London, and then New York, places I thought I'd be safe.

Somehow Mel—who had no problems with his travel but stuck by me for support—and I walked out of the security area, making eye contact with no one. We got on the plane with no problems, but as we had done on the tarmac in Jakarta, we waited on pins and needles for bad news to come. But it didn't. Nearly four hours after takeoff, we were on the ground at Heathrow Airport in London.

But the ordeal wasn't over yet.

As soon as we landed, the pilot announced over the intercom, "Everyone stay seated. No one get up."

Soon two police with automatic weapons rushed the plane. They moved with authority down both aisles of the plane, with a target clearly in mind.

My heart started pounding as I braced for them to take me off the plane. Mel turned to me: "If they're here for us, it's over. They're going to deport you back to Turkey."

I just shook my head. "Well, at this point, what can I do?"

The security forces walked down the aisle and stopped right next to my seat. *This is it*, I thought.

But as it turns out, the security personnel were looking for a man on the plane sitting right behind me who was later confirmed as an actual terrorist. I breathed a sigh of relief that the police weren't after me, and I guess it's always a good day when a known terrorist doesn't ruin your cross-continental flight. But now I had a new problem: because of the incident on the plane from Romania, our connecting flight to New York had already departed, leaving Mel and me without a way to get to New York.

An airline representative was kind to us, giving us a hotel voucher and telling us to come back the next day for the next flight. But she didn't know that I couldn't reenter the airport terminal if I left, since my passport was canceled, and I was potentially on an Interpol list. I was a man without a country.

I politely declined her offer: "I'm just going to sleep somewhere."

"What do you mean? You don't want a hotel?"

"No, I'm going to sleep at the airport." She was stunned.

Mel and I began to trudge through Heathrow Airport, one of the world's busiest, looking for a place to crash. After more than two days on the run without a change of clothes, we were pretty gross, not to mention exhausted and sick of eating airport food. Eventually we found a hotel within the airport terminal itself. Mel and I switched rooms after checking in so that if someone tried to take me from the room that was under my name, they'd have the wrong guy.

Completely mentally and physically drained after two days on the run, Mel and I dozed off immediately. After an uneventful night, we prepared to board the plane to New York the next morning. When we arrived at the gate, there was a gentleman wearing sunglasses and a baseball hat waiting for me. He spoke English, but I couldn't tell if it was with an American or British accent. He didn't have anything that identified him as being from the government or the police, as best I could tell. He didn't make much small talk, instead demanding that I hand over my green card. He examined it, took some notes, called some people, and finally said, "Go ahead." I was the only one in the boarding line who received this "special treatment" from this man, who I later learned was from the U.S. Department of Homeland Security. Just another strange event in the most tense episode of my life.

About eight hours later, the plane landed in New York. I had never been so happy to be back in the United States in my entire life. Throughout the entire ordeal, Americans were the ones helping me get back to safety: Senator Lankford. The man wearing the suit in Romania. The Department of Homeland Security agent in London. As Americans do better than anyone else in the world, they came to the rescue. I vowed that day that I would not leave American soil again until I became a U.S. citizen. And for the next four and a half years, I didn't.

My career as a human rights activist—and the sacrifices that come with it—didn't start with my time in the NBA. It all began with a promise I made to my mom, Gulsum, when I was nine years old.

I was born in Switzerland in 1992. At the time, my dad, Mehmet, was studying at the University of Zurich, and he later went on to be one of the top geneticists in Turkey. After he finished school, my family moved to Van, a city in the far eastern part of Turkey about an hour's drive from the border with Iran. This area is distant from the more cosmopolitan cities of western Turkey, such as Istanbul and Izmir, and people are less educated and more closed-minded about the world.

As a result, they are more likely to believe the kinds of false, hate-filled narratives that are common throughout the Middle East. Even before Erdoğan's Islamist regime (which is today more like a dictatorship) came to power in 2002, many Turkish news outlets were saturated with propaganda demonizing the United States, Christians, and Jews. In recent years, social media has been a new form of digital mind poison. Turkish politicians have also fed the hatred by campaigning on prejudice. Turks are extremely proud people and love officials who promise to stand up to the U.S. and European nations.

My first direct experience with how hateful people can be came when I was nine years old. One day I raced down the stairs of our apartment building to play with my friends. We were typical city kids, always playing in the street and alleys in our neighborhood. When I met up with my crew in the alley, I couldn't believe what I was seeing. My friends were burning American flags and breaking crosses.

"Guys, what are you doing?!" I cried out.

One of my friends looked up with a lighter in his hand. "What's the big deal? This is what we see people doing on TV. Americans are evil and Jews are devils."

I had no love for Americans and Jews at that time, but what my friends were doing terrified me. I was speechless. I suppose that I never believed that *my* friends, in *my* neighborhood, would imitate the same displays of venom that engulfed the world around us. They certainly weren't taught in the Kanter home, so maybe I was just sheltered.

Either way, now I had a choice to make.

Then my friend handed me the lighter. And an American flag.

"Come on, man! Burn it!"

The choice was clear: burn the flag, or lose my best friend and set myself up for years of bullying.

I threw the flag and lighter down and ran away, my friends' taunts filling my ears.

I ran up to our apartment and fell into my mom's arms.

"Mom! My friends are telling me to hate America, hate Jews, hate Christians! What do I do?"

My mom looked deep into my eyes. "I'm not going to tell you what to do. But don't hate anyone before you meet them."

She continued: "Believe in something and always stand up tall for it. Even if it means sacrificing everything you have."

That day, I made a promise to my mom. "I promise you; I am not going to hate anyone before I meet them." This promise defines my engagement with others and motivates me to speak out against injustice to this day.

Keeping that promise was easier said than done. My childhood overlapped with Erdoğan's ascendency, and over time his campaign and supporters became increasingly aggressive, injecting political Islamist and anti-American messages into their propaganda. At the same time, after the terrorist attacks of September 11, 2001, the United States entered Afghanistan and, two years later, Iraq. Many Turks (and people across the Middle East) saw this as the U.S. executing an evil plot to dominate Muslim lands—a repeat of the crusades of the Middle Ages.

Some public schools in Turkey—even elementary schools—had U.S. flags painted near the entrance so that anyone who wanted to enter had to step on them. If you didn't do it, the other kids would mock you as a traitor or a bad Muslim. Even though my parents didn't buy into the hate and lies and tried to teach us the right way, I began to believe complete myths about Jews, Christians, and Americans that I know today are totally wrong.

Besides the hate, the public schools were terrible for another reason: we students were beaten whenever we misbehaved. Every classroom had a stick that the teachers would use to hit you on the hand whenever they felt like it. Even though I was one of the better students academically and behaviorally, one day one of the teachers hit me viciously multiple times. My parents couldn't believe the bruises they saw on my hands when I came home. "That's it," my dad said. "You're out of there." The next day he came with me to school and told me to take a picture with my classmates, because it would be the last time I would see them. I never attended another public school in Turkey again.

It was then that I started going to a Hizmet ("service") school, one of many in Turkey grounded in the principles of Turkish Islamic scholar Muhammed Fethullah Gülen, who was a dear friend and teacher of mine before he died on October 20, 2024. Unlike many religious authorities in the Middle East, Gülen spent decades promoting a form of moderate

Islam characterized by tolerance, open-mindedness, and respect. Though a proud Muslim, he embraced secular government and democratic norms. It should be no surprise that his philosophy is highly popular in Turkey, a country where millions of citizens still embrace the principles of secularism on which the nation was founded in 1923 after the collapse of the Ottoman Empire.

The first time I heard about Mr. Gülen happened when I was eight years old. My mom had a huge library in the living room, and I was really into reading books. Almost every book had the same author's name on the cover: Fethullah Gülen. I remember picking up one of the books and asking my mom, "Who is this person? And why do you have so many of his books in your library?"

My mom smiled for a second and sat me in front of her. That day, she explained to me who Gülen was and what he stood for. His vision to make this world a peaceful place for people in all walks of life, his mission to educate youth, his dream of coexistence between religions, his fight against hunger, his love for interfaith dialogue, and his care for human rights for everyone, all of which were so inspiring. Even as an eight-year-old, I wanted to follow in his footsteps and advance his vision of making this world better for everyone. Eventually, Gülen's popularity made him the Turkish government's Public Enemy No. 1—with consequences for me too. But I will tell those stories later.

Being a student in one of the Hizmet schools, which exist worldwide, was a totally different experience than the one I had in the public school. For one thing, it was the first time I wasn't being taught in the classroom to hate other people. We were not indoctrinated about Gülen the man either. Instead we heard about tolerance and respect for others who are different than us. Being in a Hizmet school helped me begin to overcome the hateful attitudes I had absorbed from the toxic environment I was living in. This was just the beginning of a very long process of me overcoming my ignorance. But a new chapter in my life had begun, one that would continue later in life when I personally built a bond with Fethullah Gülen.

The other great thing about the Hizmet school was that the teachers were kind and respectful in ways the public school teachers were not. I remember sitting in class for the first time and whispering to another student, "Where's the stick?"

"What are you talking about?" he replied.

"You know, the beating stick."

He looked at me like I was crazy.

―

Although the political climate in Turkey was changing for the worse when I was a kid, I didn't pay much attention to politics or foreign affairs. What I was really focused on was playing sports.

Although I was tall, basketball was not my first love—soccer was. Like everywhere in the world outside the U.S., Turkey is soccer-crazed, and I got hooked at a young age. The problem for me was that, because I was always taller than the other kids, I was always forced to play goalie, and I hated it. I was also just too slow to be good. So I decided to take advantage of my tall stature and started playing basketball around age nine or ten.

Although there was no basketball hoop in my neighborhood in Van, that didn't stop me from working on my game. I would take a soccer ball and practice shooting it at certain spots on a stop sign, or jumping and "dunking" the ball by tapping as high as I could on the top of the sign. The other kids thought it was the most ridiculous thing they had ever seen, but I stuck with it. When I wasn't practicing, I loved watching the NBA on TV—especially the Los Angeles Lakers, led by my heroes Shaquille O'Neal and Kobe Bryant. I would often wake up at three or four in the morning and sneak into the living room to watch them play. I timed everything perfectly so that if my mom ever awoke from her sleep to be sure I was really in bed, I could slip back into my room undetected. Moments later, when she went back to bed, I would turn it back on and keep watching the game.

Originally, the biggest barrier to success on the basketball court was my parents, who didn't want me to play at all. They always preached the importance of excelling in school, and they feared that a commitment to sports would take away from my academic performance. But I really liked playing ball, and I constantly nagged them to let me play. My physical education teacher, Fatih Karali, was in their ear too—he saw something promising in me.

Finally, one day, when I was ten years old, my dad told me, "If you can beat me one-on-one, I'll let you play." For the next two months I practiced tirelessly, preparing for the day when I would challenge my dad. Then, one Saturday, we walked to my school's basketball hoop and started playing. I beat him fair and square. He kept his promise and told me, "I respect your dedication and hard work. I'll let you do it. But you need to promise me one thing: whatever happens, you need to be a good student before a good ballplayer. School comes first." That sounded fair to me.

With Fatih coaching me, my game began to blossom. He instructed me on fundamentals and was the first person to ever tell me that I could play in the NBA someday. His confidence translated into my confidence. I applied so much of what he taught me at every step of my career, and we are still friends today.

My family lived in Van until I was about fourteen years old. At that time, my parents were eager to move to a part of Turkey where the people had greater levels of education and refinement, but they weren't sure where to go. One day in the spring of 2006, my dad, who is a giant himself at 6'5", was on a trip to Ankara, the nation's capital, and went into an office supply store. A guy, who assumed my dad had children, came up to him and asked if he had a son who was going to be as tall as he was.

"Yeah," my dad said. "He's almost taller than me!"

"Bring him here to Ankara so he can start training with a real basketball club," the man said. "He could have a bright future."

When my dad got home from his trip, he sat me down. "This guy I met in Ankara wants you to play ball for his club," he told me. "How do you feel about moving there?"

"Absolutely!"

That summer my dad and I went back to Ankara for a week to make sure the situation was as good as it seemed, and I worked out for a club called Efes—one of the very best in Turkey. At the first practice, it was clear that I was already better than every other kid my age, despite barely playing organized basketball. Everyone was mystified how this guy—me—emerged from the middle of nowhere in eastern Turkey to be so good. People ask me all the time how I got to be so talented at the game. There is no question I worked hard at it. But more than anything, God gave me a natural gift.

Everything was going great—or so it seemed. But then, as would happen so many times over the course of my career, I hit a setback. My dad and I were staying at the Efes coach's house. My parents are very religious people who don't drink alcohol. Unfortunately, one night the coach held up a beer in front of my dad and said, "I can't get to sleep at night if I don't drink one of these." I took one look at my dad's face and knew this would be a problem. Later, in private, he told me, "There's no way you're going to this club!" I think he was afraid I would take up similar habits.

I was crushed and started crying. I begged my parents to let me go. Eventually they relented, but my mom had one condition: I had to go to one of the Hizmet schools in Ankara.

"I'll do anything you want!" I pleaded. "I just want to play basketball!"

Later that summer, when I was fourteen, the Kanter family moved to Ankara. My parents weren't thrilled about me playing basketball in the first place, so I give them enormous credit for making a decision that would allow me to pursue my dream. Going to Ankara was also good for me personally. I was pretty shy as a kid, and all I knew in Van was my own little neighborhood and the people I went to school with. In Ankara I began to come out of my shell as I learned how to engage with my teammates and coaches.

While preparing to play for Efes, my academic career started at Samanyolu College, another Hizmet school. I hoped to earn an athletic scholarship by making the basketball team. The coach, Halil Ercikti, gave me a tryout. "I'll give you a few shots," he said. "If you make them, I'll give you a scholarship." This was a completely ridiculous way to award a scholarship, but I wasn't about to complain. I went three-for-three, and it was a done deal. If only everything in life was so easy.

Then came some terrible news about my eligibility to play—something that would become a pattern in my basketball career.

There is a weird law in Turkey that an amateur basketball player can play for only one team at a time. I had no idea about this law when I agreed to play for Samanyolu, which meant I was suddenly ineligible to play for the far superior Efes club. As soon as I heard this, I exploded that Samanyolu had tricked me (they hadn't). Fortunately, the Efes coach was very calm and understanding about the situation. "This is the best school team in Ankara. We'll let him play here," he said. "He'll develop his game, and then we'll put him on our senior team when he gets old enough."

Samanyolu gave me a chance to play with talented players against challenging competition. But Coach Ercikti was a drill sergeant. I was one of the best players on the team, but he cut me after the fifth or sixth game. I continued with the team as a lowly water boy for a few games, completely upset and confused why he made this decision. Later on, I realized that he did it to keep me humble. I was thriving on the court, and he didn't want me to start getting cocky and start coasting. Once he put me back on the team, he and the other coaches were very positive and warned me not to get distracted and urged me to always give 100 percent.

By the end of my freshman year, I had shot up in height to about 6'9". One day I was at a tournament, watching some games played by other age groups before my team hit the court. A round-faced man of about forty, wearing black shorts and a red T-shirt, was sitting next to me. I had never met him before. He asked who I played for, and I told him.

"Do you know who I am?" he asked me.

"No, I'm sorry," I replied.

"My name is Mustafa Derin. I'm the coach for Turkey's sixteen-and-under national team."

Mustafa and I talked for about an hour, forging an instant bond. His basketball IQ was superb.

"Can you dunk?" he also asked me.

"Yeah."

"When you play, show me."

When my team took the court to play in the tournament, I played a great game, but the opportunity to dunk didn't arise naturally within the flow of the game. So, when the final buzzer sounded, I lingered on the court as the teams went back into the locker room. I took the ball from the ref's hands, sprinted down the court, and slammed the ball through the basket. Mustafa saw it and gave me a nod. When I reconnected with him again at the end of the day, he told me, "I'm going to bring you to practice for the national team in Ankara. If you're good, you'll make the team."

My heart leapt at such an amazing opportunity. A week later, I scrimmaged with the team, and played well. Not long after, Derin sent me an invite to the actual training camp, and I made the team. (The strange Turkish "one team at a time" law doesn't apply to the national team, apparently.) Not only that, but I was dominating sixteen-year-olds as a fifteen-year-old. Later that week, Samanyolu's principal announced to the whole school that I was the newest member of the national team. Shock waves rippled through the school at the news that this quiet newcomer was one of the best basketball players in the country.

I began practicing with my new teammates on the national team as we prepared to challenge the best talent from around the world. One of the most memorable aspects of my time with the 16-and-under team was our matchups with the junior national teams from Greece and Serbia. Turkey has a very tense history with both of these nations. For centuries the Ottoman Empire ruled over modern-day Greece and Serbia. The higher-ups in the Turkish national team organization used the history of ethnic conflict to fire us up before the games, telling us we would be heroes in Turkey if we won. Filled with this toxic motivation, we screamed and slammed doors in the locker room before the game. I could tell that the Greek and Serbian coaches were using the same motivational strategy on their kids too, because our opponents played harder against us than I saw them do against other teams.

As you would expect, the contests against these countries were at times more like street fights than basketball games. Many times, we shouted curse words in Greek or Serbian at our opponents, words we had looked up on the internet before the game. As a result, a brawl almost broke out in one game against Serbia. In Greece, the environment was downright dangerous. The fans in the stands waved knives in our faces—we couldn't believe they were threatening to cut fifteen- and sixteen-year-old kids! Nor could we ever walk in the streets in Greece with our Turkish national team shirts on. When going out in groups, we were instructed to tell anyone who asked that we were from Bulgaria or Georgia. It's this kind of senseless hatred that I am now living to combat.

Because of my time with the national team, serious basketball people in Turkey were now keeping an eye on my progress and were telling me and my parents that I had the potential to be good enough to play professionally. One Turkish team, Ülker, was urging me to come play for them.

But to do that, the Ülker representatives said, my journey had to continue in Istanbul.

CHAPTER 2

THE GREAT ESCAPE

We'd been battling each other for years. This game would finally prove to the scouts who was better.

Jonas Valanciunas and I were born two weeks apart in the same year. Like me, the Lithuanian center towered over everyone and dominated most competition with ease. Beginning when we both played for our under-16 national teams, we constantly faced off against one another in international matchups, banging against one another in the post to claim the title as the best young big man in Europe. By the time we got to be seventeen years old, we heard the scouts debating with each other: "Which one would you take in the NBA draft?"

That question was about to be answered at the 2009 Europe Under-18 Championship in France.

Coming into the annual tournament, everyone in the basketball world was eager to see Jonas and me face off in the title game. He and I were destroying everyone in the group stage and quarterfinals, and we looked set to collide in the final. But it wasn't to be. Although I put up 32 points and 25 rebounds in the semifinal game against Serbia, the Serbs took us down, and Lithuania fell to France in their contest. Still, that meant that Turkey would play Lithuania for third place.

This game was legendary—the most intense of my life to date. Throughout the game, both sides' fans were chanting our names (and screaming insults). I was motivated to show everyone that I was the best young player in Europe. Jonas had the same goal. He and I went back and forth the entire game. At the end, the scoreboard read 95–74 in Turkey's favor. Even though I was a year younger than almost everyone, I played out of my mind, scoring 35 points and grabbing 19 rebounds, while also posting 4 blocks. That performance made me the MVP of the entire tournament, even though Turkey didn't even play for the championship. It also set the scouts on fire that I could be a top NBA draft pick.

A year before the 2009 European under-18 championship, my family relocated to Istanbul, the largest city in Turkey and the cultural capital of the nation. There was a sole purpose to this move: I was positioning myself to be a professional basketball player. My dad, who initially didn't even want me to play basketball, was enthusiastically supportive. But my highly religious mom was terrified that I'd go to Istanbul—a city of 16 million that is nearly three times the size of Ankara—and get caught up in vices such as drinking, drugs, and clubbing. She forbade me from going. I was by this time about 6'9", but I was still a kid. My size didn't stop me from bursting into tears, through which I told my mom that she was ruining my career. Eventually we reached another deal: I would stay one more year in Ankara, and then I'd go to Istanbul. Another year went by, but my parents kept their word. I will always be grateful to them for their willingness to uproot their lives to help me succeed.

The team that had pursued me the hardest, Ülker, had recently merged with a club called Fenerbahçe. The basketball team is just one part of the Fenerbahçe sports empire, which has its home in the Kadıköy district of Istanbul. Although the soccer team is Fenerbahçe's crown jewel, the basketball team is also extremely popular and has won the second-most titles in the history of the Turkish basketball league. Bojan Bogdanović, Thabo Sefolosha, Ömer Aşık, Mahmoud Abdul-Rauf, and many other notable players have all suited up for the team, which is also competitive in the EuroLeague, the NBA of Europe, where all the top clubs in Europe play one another.

When I first signed with the team, I was proud to be wearing the Fenerbahçe jersey. But, like many sports clubs outside the U.S., Fenerbahçe had a sleazy side. In 2013, for example, the soccer team was banned from competing in the European Champions League because of a match-fixing scandal among team players and executives. Fenerbahçe was fond of using strong-arm tactics to control its players. There were also rumors of connections to organized crime.

During the day I attended Fenerbahçe's school for athletes (and some regular kids were enrolled too). The schedule was mostly the same as a normal school day, but sometimes I got tapped to practice or play with the senior team and could leave early. Nobody else on the squad was my age. I trained hard with the club and developed my skills further, but I didn't see the court much in official games. And even though I was 6'9" as a sixteen-year-old, I didn't have enough of the strength or experience to earn major minutes against grown men, some of whom had been playing professionally for fifteen years or more. But practicing against the guys was invaluable for improving my game. The choice was to either get good enough to compete with them or have a second-rate career.

I did have a few great moments wearing Fenerbahçe's jersey. In my first game in the EuroLeague, I had a dunk against the German club Alba Berlin that threw the fans into a frenzy. In that moment, I realized that I wasn't a kid anymore. I was a professional, capable of one day becoming a player who could hold my own against the best competition anywhere. The second thought that came into my mind after that was more sobering: *Basketball is going to be my life from now on. It's a job now. Whatever comes my way, I have to accept it and adjust.*

Of course, having a job means getting paid. Since I was still in high school, I did not cash in big from Fenerbahçe. But the club did pay housing and living expenses for me and my family, and gave me a small salary on top of it. After I got my first check, I took all my friends to Pizza Hut and purchased a deal offering unlimited pizza.

During my first year with the club, I had an opportunity to travel to Greece for a Jordan Brand camp with some of the best players in Europe. It was there that I met the legendary basketball trainer Tim Grover, who has personally trained some of the biggest names in NBA history, including Kobe Bryant, Dwyane Wade, and His Airness himself, Michael Jordan. Someone had told me that Tim trained MJ, so all camp I looked for an opportunity to talk to him. Tim loved my game and gave me some advice that would change my life: "If you stay in Turkey, they're going to make you sign a long-term contract. You won't come to the NBA until you're twenty-two or twenty-three. At that point, you'll be behind in your development, and you won't know any English to communicate and bond with your teammates. Your whole career is going to be affected. Come to America as soon as possible."

I locked what Tim said away in my mind and started contemplating my future. I knew I wanted to go to the NBA, and the fact that someone like Tim thought I had what it took was thrilling. In the meantime, since I performed well at the camp in Greece, Nike invited me to be part of the first-ever international team at the Jordan Brand Classic in New York City—one of the most prestigious tournaments in the U.S. for high school players. I still thought the U.S. would corrupt my entire belief system, so I was nervous to set foot on American soil. Additionally, many Turks will harass people who visit countries they don't like, such as the United States, Greece, or Armenia. "You aren't a real Turk," they'd say. "You're a lapdog." I didn't want my teammates to think about me this way if I went.

I had a conversation about my fears with my parents, who said, "If you are serious about succeeding in basketball, you have to travel to New York. You aren't moving there. It's five days. Check it out." Nike had assembled a highly structured program for me and other international players, so I'd be in a basketball bubble. In the end, I dismissed my fears of not being able to handle fame, or what my Fenerbahçe teammates would think, and bravely went ahead.

Immediately upon arrival in New York, I instantly realized how much I needed to work on my English. I also didn't know what to expect from Americans, so I kept totally to myself, not even wanting to engage with them. Astonishingly, my coach for the week, Raphael Chillious, was really kind to me, making sure that I had halal food (food that is prepared in accordance with Islamic law) to eat, and that my sixteen-year-old growing body always got its fill of it. I was confused—in a good way. *Why is this Black American guy trying to make sure a Muslim is fed enough?* I wondered. It was my first experience of seeing what I now see every day: more often than not, Americans are quick to extend kindness across racial and ethnic lines.

Being in New York City was an electric experience. I was captivated by the grandeur of the skyscrapers blanketing the tiny island of Manhattan and the energy pulsing from the city's busy streets. The Jordan Brand staffers exposed us to the city's highlights, taking us to the Statue of Liberty, the Empire State Building, and some ritzy restaurants. Then they took us to a Knicks game at Madison Square Garden. The raucous energy the crowd brought to cheering for the Knicks, even though they were a dismal team back then, made intense European arenas look almost sleepy. *This is where I want to play someday*, I vowed to myself. *I would die to play for this team.* The desire to play in New York overwhelmed the fear of devils.

One thing I was certainly not excited about was my roommate situation. The camp organizers had arranged for a guy from Turkey to chaperone me. He was there to make sure I understood everything that was being said in English and navigate any other problems that might come up. My first night there he told me, "We might have a little problem."

"Why is that?"

"You have a roommate."

"So what?"

"His name is Tomer Bar-Even."

"And?"

"He's from Israel."

Harboring a severe mistrust of Jews, I instantly demanded, "You need to change it immediately. I don't even want to play if he's my roommate."

"We can't do anything about it—we don't control the assignments."

"There's no way."

"Look, it's only for four days. Just deal with it."

The next day, Tomer, who came a day late, walked into the room for the first time when I happened to be there. He put down his bags and tried to shake my hand. I didn't say a word, not even a hello, and gave him a lethargic fist bump instead of a real handshake. For the next few days, we coexisted in an icy silence. I didn't even want to be in the room with him—I would hang out in the lobby as late as possible so that he'd be asleep by the time I returned. I'd also wake up early and leave before he even got up, and use the bathroom in the lobby, just so we didn't have to interact.

On the court, I played a complete game in the game for international players, posting a double double (double-digit points and rebounds) against some of the best players my age in Europe (including Jonas). Despite my rudeness at the hotel, my roommate, Tomer, a point guard, consistently fed me the ball. The fact that he didn't let my obnoxious behavior stand in the way of a team effort was a humbling experience. After the game, in the locker room, I mumbled "I'm sorry" to him in broken English and shook his hand. I don't recall what he said, but I'm confident he understood that I was trying to make amends. But I still resolved not to tell anyone that I shook a Jewish person's hand.

At the conclusion of the week, Coach Chillious, then an assistant coach for the University of Washington Huskies, told me, "We really want you at Washington." That was the first program that was in any way interested in me playing for them. Between my desire to polish my game in college and the priority my parents put on education, it was easy to immediately tell him yes. On the final day of camp, Kevin Durant, then the superstar forward for the Seattle SuperSonics (which later became the Oklahoma City Thunder), made an appearance and gave a speech. I was starstruck. Little did I know that I would be his teammate six years later. Perhaps most memorable of all, at the end of the camp I got to meet everyone's all-time basketball hero, Michael Jordan. Shaking his hand helped fuel my hunger to continue my future as a basketball player in the United States.

But Fenerbahçe wasn't as excited as I was about it.

Almost immediately after I returned to Turkey from the Jordan Brand Classic in New York, Fenerbahçe offered me a lucrative contract: six years for about $6 million. They had heard how I had dominated in the tournament and planned to develop me into their next star. The Greek team Olympiacos, one of the very best in Europe, also offered me a fortune to come play for them. That was a life-changing amount of money for anyone, let alone a sixteen-year-old kid. Teammates, friends, and coaches all urged me to sign the contract. If I took this deal, it seemed like things would play out in the way Tim Grover warned me about. Then I asked my dad what he thought.

"Don't take it," he said calmly. "I know this sounds too good to pass up. But if you stay here, you're going to be just another one of them. You have to get an education. And the political environment is getting more toxic here in Turkey."

I told Fenerbahçe that I planned to leave the team and move to the United States to play my final two years of high school. The bosses exploded at the news and threatened me: "If you go to America, then we will make sure that you don't play a second. You'll never see the court." Mirsad Türkcan, a star player on the team who was also the first Turkish player in the NBA, literally took off his shoes and threw them at me when he saw me—a grave insult in the Middle East.

"How could you even think about going to the U.S. without asking me?!" he roared.

"Dude, you're not my agent!" I fired back. It was weird that he thought he had the right to control me like that.

Throughout the year, Fenerbahçe kept pressuring me to take the deal, making it even sweeter by telling me that the team would rename the new basketball arena it was building after me. The enormous pressure from other people continued as well. My coach on the national team sat me down and told me to write out $6 million on paper. I wrote a six with five zeros: $600,000.

"That's only six hundred thousand," he said. "Add another zero."

Six million dollars. My family and I would be set for life! Again I consulted my dad and told him, "We have to take this!"

"No, we don't," he responded.

When the season ended, and with my desire to go to America still strong, the chief financial officer of the entire Fenerbahçe organization, Mahmut Uslu, summoned me to his office in the Şükrü Saracoğlu Stadium, the team's soccer arena. Once I sat down, he shoved a piece of paper across his desk at me.

"Look at this."

The paper contained a list of names. I had no idea who they were.

"What is this?"

"These are the names of all the players who left Turkey to play in the U.S. and failed. Do you want me to add your name?"

I looked down at the paper, insulted at his lack of confidence in me. I told myself, *I'm definitely going now. I'm going to prove them wrong.*

That wasn't the worst threat that Fenerbahçe, which operates more like a mafia family than a business, made to me. The bosses told me that if I went to the U.S., they would send my payment records to the media and make me ineligible to play at the college level.

That threat of blackmail pushed me over the edge. There was no way I was re-signing with these criminals.

I went home and started packing to leave Turkey that very day. In some ways, I had no choice but to leave. Fenerbahçe had also leaked to the media that I had rejected such a rich contract, and the fans were furious. Some started roaming around my neighborhood hunting for me. My mom and dad begged me not to even leave the house. But there was no turning back, even as I maintained fears that America would cause me to abandon my faith and my culture.

My most valuable partner in my escape was a friend named Max. Max is a Turkish sports agent known for helping bring Turkish players to the U.S. We had gotten acquainted over the past several months, and he had asked Tim Grover if he would be willing to train me if I ever wanted to come to the U.S. Tim was delighted to say yes. Now it was time for me to accept Tim's offer.

On my last day in Turkey, I went to the dentist for a checkup before I left for America. Then my mom cooked a huge meal of my favorite foods: Turkish rice, *fasulye* (green bean and meat stew), and *çiğ köfte* (spiced raw meatballs). For dessert, we had a tasty *aşure* pudding. I didn't know it at the time, but that would be the last time I ate dinner with my entire family around the table.

The next morning, we said our goodbyes. My mom hugged me and gave me some *börek*—a Turkish spinach and feta cheese pastry—to go. I rolled my eyes, but mothers always want to make sure their sons are fed. "Don't eat too many burgers and fries and get fat," my sister Betül joked, knowing my appetite for fast food. My brother Kerem, three years younger than me, hoped to come to the U.S. for his whole high school career. "Hold it down for me, and I'll see you in a year," he vowed. My littlest brother, Ahmet, who was only eight or nine at the time, gave me a little card and told me, "Read it when you get to America."

My dad drove me—wearing a hat and sunglasses to conceal my identity from the crazy fans who might want to hurt me—to the airport. As I hugged him and said goodbye, he told me, "I'm proud of you, son. Whether you make it or fail, your family has your back no matter what." This poured jet fuel on my motivation to make it to the NBA. I had turned down millions to go into an unknown situation. I knew I could always come back, but I wanted to make the family who believed in me proud.

Outside the gate, I met Max, who was also wearing a hat and sunglasses and acted like he was reading a newspaper so no one could see his face. With him was another player Max was bringing to the U.S. on this day, a teammate named Kevin Kaspar. I first met Kevin when we both played on the Turkish under-18 team and roomed together. When I saw him take off his shirt, I noticed that he was wearing a cross.

"Oh my God!" I gasped. "You're not Muslim!"

It was true. Although Kevin was a Turkish national, he was of Armenian ethnicity and a Christian. But much to my surprise, Kevin had defied the stereotypes I developed in my mind about Armenians and Christians—he was a good guy and became a friend. He was also an ace floor general at the point guard position, and his high skill level meant Max was eager to bring Kevin to the U.S. at the same time he brought me. The plan was for us to play together and dominate, wherever we ended up.

The plane was delayed on the tarmac for an hour or so. I panicked, thinking that someone from Fenerbahçe had pulled some strings with the government to stop me from leaving the country. Eventually the plane took off, and I exhaled a monumental sigh of relief. At the same time, sitting in my seat, my mind started to fill with anxiety about what lay on the other side. A short visit to America—my trip to New York—was one thing. But living in America was another. In my mind, where people hated Islam and Muslims. It was a place where faithful Muslims—as I tried to be—get pressured into a lifestyle against their values. Even though I had consumed information in books and YouTube videos that suggested my misconceptions weren't true, I still was not totally convinced about the nature of America.

Six thousand miles later, my plane touched down at Chicago O'Hare International Airport. I barely knew anyone in the U.S. My English was embarrassing. And I was still just a kid, only seventeen years old. In other words, I was like millions of other immigrants who have come to America over the centuries. That night, as I munched on my mom's *börek*, I read the card Ahmet had drawn me. It was a crayon drawing of me and him together, captioned with a child's precious words: "Good luck with your basketball career. I'm praying for you."

After getting settled at Max's house in Chicago—which would become my home for the next few months—my first mission was to go to Tim Grover's gym on the south side of Chicago. Grover's gym is a famous place for high-level hoopers to practice and play pickup ball. I meekly walked in, not speaking to or even making eye contact with anyone. After all, I was brand-new in the country, paralyzed with fear about what to expect. What I didn't anticipate seeing was the scene on the court: both NBA players and top-level high school and college guys playing 5-on-5.

Grover greeted me and told me to get dressed.

"What for?"

"You're going to get in the game against these guys."

My eyes bulged, and Tim noticed how shocked and intimidated I was.

"How else are you going to get better unless you play against people better than you?" Tim asked. Good point.

My head was spinning. This was my second day in America, I was seventeen, and I was being told to go play against NBA stars. I got into the game and had a good, hard run (even though I still didn't make eye contact or talk with my teammates). Over the course of the summer, I'd eventually play against NBA megastars like LeBron, Kevin Durant, and Derrick Rose in Grover's state-of-the-art facility. But my favorite part about Grover's gym was something I discovered on my very first day: his huge fridge full of Muscle Milk—a delicious post-workout protein shake.

"How much is each one?" I asked Tim on the first day.

He looked at me funny. "It's all free!"

America was living up to its reputation as a land of abundance! I started chugging Muscle Milk every ten or fifteen minutes on my first day.

After my first workout, I silently darted back into the locker room, avoiding any interaction. I quickly collected my belongings, trying to escape as fast as possible. I didn't even bother to shower.

Then two of my teammates—both high-level players about my age, whose names I don't remember today—approached me. They started to introduce themselves, but I scurried out of the locker room.

A few steps outside the door, my conscience stopped me dead in my tracks as I once again remembered the promise to my mom. I couldn't write these guys off before I got to know them. I sheepishly went back in and approached them.

I took a deep breath. "What's up?"

"We know that you just came from Turkey yesterday. We've been following your game. You're a really good player!"

That was kind of them to say. But I was painfully shy and embarrassed by my English. All I could manage was, "Okay."

"We know that you're Muslim. We know a couple of mosques that we can take you to. And if you want to go get some halal food, we know a couple of the best spots."

"Okay," I mumbled.

I couldn't believe what I was hearing. It was the opposite of everything I had heard in the last seventeen years back home. I decided to go with them. These guys—who I later learned were Christians—took me to a mosque and respectfully waited outside as I prayed. Then we got some halal food. I was dreading eating it, and even wondered if my new "friends" were trying to deceive me. I asked them, "Is this really halal or are you just trying to make me eat pork?"

They laughed. "No, look, this is the sign on the door! It says fully halal, one hundred percent!"

Maybe Americans weren't so bad, after all.

CHAPTER 3

THE NEW WORLD

My first summer after arriving in the U.S., in 2009, was an extraordinary time of learning. The buildings were huge, everything was expensive, and people of different races mostly coexisted peacefully (which is not really the case in Turkey with Turks and Kurds). This was also my first time living around Christians and Jews, and I felt very uneasy.

Additionally, I had never been around Black people in my life. One day some friends and I were in a Louis Vuitton store in downtown Chicago (not that I had any money to buy anything). Out of pure curiosity over what Black skin felt like, I decided to approach a total stranger in the store and touch his skin—without even asking! Needless to say, this experiment did not go over well. This perplexed man gawked at me and exclaimed, "What are you doing?!"

"I was just saying hi."

A friend came to my rescue and explained the situation. "He's a brand-new foreigner in this country. I'm really sorry about that." I was lucky I didn't get knocked out.

But as much as I was learning off the court, my focus remained on what I was in the United States to do on it. This was the main reason I had left everything behind in Turkey.

So imagine my surprise when I learned that I wasn't allowed to play.

Over the summer of 2009, while I stayed at his house and trained at Tim Grover's gym, Max had advised me to play my senior-year season at Findlay Prep, a school in Henderson, Nevada. It's common for the very best high school players in the U.S. to travel far from their homes to play ball at schools that can showcase their talent. Findlay, which closed in 2019, was essentially a basketball factory. NBA players such as Dillon Brooks, P. J. Washington, Avery Bradley, Kelly Oubre Jr., and many others played high school ball there. Findlay traveled the country playing top competition, and had gone 33–0 the year before I arrived, finishing as the top-ranked high school team in the nation and winning a national championship. I couldn't wait to showcase my skills for top college coaches who would be watching. Plus, I'd be playing on a stacked team with future pros Tristan Thompson and Cory Joseph. I thought we had a chance to go down as the best high school team ever.

But things didn't go according to plan.

Right before my high school season started, Tim called me and Max into his office at his gym in Chicago around 5 or 6 p.m.—a very unusual time for a meeting with him.

"We have a huge problem," he began. "Nike heard you left Turkey and came to the U.S. They are emailing everyone—coaches, leagues, schools, the NCAA—saying that you are a pro and have a shoe deal. They're telling everyone to not let you play in your league." Apparently, Nike, which intended for me to be their next big star in Europe, wasn't pleased with my change of plans.

I knew that Nike had sent me tons of free apparel when I played for Fenerbahçe. But it was a surprise to me that I had a shoe deal. Shockingly, Tim told me that my dad had signed a deal on my behalf when I was around sixteen, without my knowledge. Even though I had nothing to do with it, this created a serious problem, because in those days amateurs who got compensated were at risk of being ineligible to play at the high school or college level.

As soon as other coaches read Nike's emails and discovered that I had competed in the EuroLeague with Fenerbahçe, they branded me as a professional. Coaches at the most elite schools across the country whose teams would have to play against Findlay Prep started saying publicly that I was a pro who should not be allowed to play. If I did play, their teams would refuse to take the court against us. The ringleader was Steve Smith, head coach at the famous Oak Hill Academy in Virginia.

The coach at Findlay, Michael Peck, was hopeful I could still suit up for his team. But after I practiced with the team for three weeks, he called Max and told him to come to Nevada as soon as possible. Later that night, I eavesdropped on Coach Peck and Max talking quietly at Coach's home. With my ear pressed against the door, I heard Coach Peck say, "His dad signed a deal. I don't think he's ever going to be able to play high school ball in America."

I eased away from the door and sat on the stairs, burying my head in my hands. I had turned down millions to come to America, and now I couldn't even play. Then I called my dad to ask him about the shoe deal.

He didn't deny it. "Please don't be mad at me, son," my dad pleaded. "I just wanted to do what's best for you. I didn't know the rules in America. This is not your fault; this is my fault. I'm sorry for doing something behind your back without asking you." It was a simple case of a good man trying to make a smart financial decision for his son and his family, since our middle-class family got free Nike gear for life and a good bit of money out of it. Sadly, it backfired.

I released the phone out of my hand and let it drop to the floor in despair, disbelief, and frustration. Then I managed to pick it back up. "That's okay," I muttered to my dad. "I'll fight through this."

A tragic element to this situation was how my friend Kevin Kaspar was dragged through it. The plan of us being a dynamic duo was now in shambles, and it felt like it was all my fault. Max told Kevin, "You can stay here, but I need to move Enes somewhere else where he might be eligible."

Kevin didn't flinch. "Enes is my best friend. I came here with him. And I'm sticking with him."

A school called Mountain State Academy in West Virginia was still willing to take a chance on me, so I packed what few clothes I had in my luggage and flew with Max and Kevin across the country to Beckley, West Virginia, a coal-mining town of about 17,000. Brand-new in town, I started practicing with the team. With no guarantees that I'd ever see the court in a real high school game, the gym was filled with college coaches trying to get what might be their only look at me. Like Findlay, Mountain State closed its doors in 2010. It was a school in name only, and I'm sure my parents would not have been happy had they known how unserious the academics were.

Sadly, it is a common practice in the elite ranks of American high school basketball for advisers to shuffle players from school to school with little regard for whether they are being prepared well for life beyond basketball. Not everyone will achieve the dream of going to the NBA. Moreover, the basketball life can be an enormous strain on human beings who look like grown men but are still teenagers. It is extremely difficult for anyone to focus completely on basketball and navigate the pressures that come with it—coaches, finances, college eligibility, media attention, scouts, and more. But it is nothing short of overwhelming for a kid to do it.

West Virginia was a strange place for a newcomer to America. My previous experiences in the U.S. had been almost entirely in New York, Chicago, and the suburbs of Las Vegas. The mountains of West Virginia weren't exactly the big city. My English was still pathetic, and the locals' thick country accents didn't help me get better. I lived with an American family that drank Dr Pepper with breakfast every morning—a level of soda consumption that definitely doesn't happen in Turkey. My West Virginia "mother" also warned me not to go outside after dark because of dangerous animals in the forest. "Where *are* we?" Kevin and I would wonder out loud to each other.

Soon enough, the episode that occurred at Findlay repeated itself at Mountain State. The Mountain State coach summoned Max and me to campus and broke the news to us: Enes won't be able to play. I was beside myself with exasperation. It was bad enough I couldn't play here, but I also couldn't go back to Turkey. Every club there would use me as the poster child for failure, a warning for every young Turkish player who ever wanted to come to the U.S.

Max had one final option: a small school outside Los Angeles called Stoneridge Prep. NBA players Taj Gibson and Nikola Vucevic had both attended there and on to play at the University of Southern California, so I figured it couldn't be that bad. Once again I had the conversation with Kevin: "I don't want to drag you everywhere with me." And again Kevin held firm: "I'm your best friend. You're my best friend. I came to America to play with you, so I want to move there with you." His loyalty meant everything to me at a very lonely time. I was happy to see him later go on to play Division I basketball at Western Kentucky. But sadly, like so many former friends and teammates, Kevin no longer speaks to me out of fear of the Turkish government making his life miserable for associating with me.

With no other option to keep myself on the court, I enrolled at Stoneridge. When people think of a prep school in Simi Valley, they probably think of a gorgeous campus with affluent students in one of the nicest parts of Southern California. But Stoneridge had only about fifteen players crammed into miserable facilities, with spiders and other insects crawling around the classroom. While I was grateful to have a school where I could play ball, the level of competition in the prep school league was pathetic. I was consistently scoring 40 or 50 points per game against small players from tiny schools. It might sound great to be dominating, but I needed to improve my game so that I would be ready to excel against top competition in college. I wasn't getting any better.

Off the court, life was thoroughly depressing. Simi Valley's practice facility was a court at a 24 Hour Fitness gym, where we had to fight for court space against random old men who insisted on their right to shoot some jumpers on this public court (and they had a fair point). My living conditions were also a cause for misery. I originally lived in a two-bedroom apartment with four other guys. Kevin and I shared a room, and I squeezed into a little twin bed with my feet hanging over the edge. In the living room was one couch and a small TV. When our clothes got dirty, we hauled our laundry down the street to a laundromat to wash and dry them. We barely had any money, and whenever we went grocery shopping, we inhaled all the food before it even got put away. One time, I poured milk into a bowl of Cheez-Its, thinking they were cereal. Whenever I opened the fridge, all I saw was half-empty bottles of ketchup, ranch, and barbecue sauce—try to feed five 17–18-year-old athletes with just that. In my downtime, I tried to learn English by watching *SpongeBob SquarePants*.

I started to question why I had come to America at all. As a player in Turkey, I had my own masseuse at age sixteen. I turned down a $6 million contract from one of the top teams in Europe. Now, far away from home, with no money, I was eating Nutella-and-bread for breakfast, lunch, and dinner. At the same time, Fenerbahçe kept sending me messages on Facebook, gloating over my failures and trying to lure me back to the team.

I tried to hide how hard life was from my parents, but Max was quietly filling them in. They knew I wasn't getting a great education at Stoneridge, and that especially distressed my mom. When I did talk with my parents, about every two weeks, I tried not to say anything that would make them sad. Still, they blamed themselves for my entire predicament: "This is our fault! How could we have done this to you?"

"Just keep seeing the big picture," Max kept encouraging me. But it was difficult to tune it all out and focus on my goal of playing for a Division I NCAA team, and eventually the NBA.

"What big picture? I turned down millions to come to a school covered with spiders!"

I tried to console myself with the thought that I'd soon be on campus at a prestigious NCAA D-I program, which would basically be considered a professional atmosphere anywhere else in the world. Additionally, my family discouraged me from coming back to Turkey, because Fenerbahçe continued to smear my reputation in the Turkish media, and the threat of violence from their most unhinged supporters was very real.

Eventually, partly because Stoneridge had trouble paying rent on the apartment, some teammates and I moved in with an American family, the Barrys. Mike and Kristin, and their three kids, had gotten connected with Stoneridge when they saw us players working out at the 24 Hour Fitness. When they saw how we were living in the crummy apartment, they asked our coach to let a few of us live with them. When I approached their spacious home for the first time, I noticed that they had an American flag in front, which was unusual to me (most Turks don't fly the national flag for any reason).

"What is this?"

"It's an American flag."

"I know, but is your house, like, an embassy?"

They smiled. "No, we love our country, so we have this flag in front of our house."

I thought it was bizarre that they displayed the Stars and Stripes in front of their home. Little did I know how precious that flag would later become to me.

In contrast to the tiny apartment I was sharing, the Barry home—which became a basketball boardinghouse—was very comfortable, and I had all I wanted to eat. The Barrys even drove us to school and to practice. But one thing disturbed me. In my bedroom there was a cross hanging on the wall over my bed. *Oh my God*, I thought. *They want to convert me to Christianity!* So, the second night I was there I crept out of bed, took the cross off the wall, and broke it. Then I hid the busted pieces of wood somewhere I thought the family wouldn't find them.

The next day, Kristin noticed my act of religious desecration. She was furious, yelling, "Who broke my cross?" I didn't say a word. I was terrified the family would kick me out of their house, and then I'd literally be homeless. It wasn't hard to discern who had committed the crime, but I guess they figured I was just a young kid from the Middle East whose mind had been poisoned at an early age and so didn't know any better. They let it go, never even mentioning it.

That was just one moment when the Barrys were very patient with me. Kristin had to reassure me that her chocolate chip cookies didn't have alcohol in them. One teammate played a prank on me, telling me that American girls like to be called "chubby" as a compliment. My "sister" in the Barry home didn't think it was so funny when I called her that. But we all learned to live together. In time, I became comfortable enough to call Kristin "Mom." I have nothing but praise and gratitude for the Barrys and how they treated me, and I still maintain a friendship with them to this day.

My first year in America also provided a couple of important learning experiences about American diversity and traditions. Nothing tops the list like my first Thanksgiving.

A friend named Billy in Chicago, where I returned while on Thanksgiving break, invited me to his family's house for Thanksgiving dinner. This friend wasn't just a Christian—at the time, a cause for distrust in my uneducated mind. I thought that Thanksgiving was potentially a dangerous affair—who knows what evil practices the Americans did there? Something might happen that would cause me to lose my Muslim faith entirely.

American. Christian. Thanksgiving. To my immature mind, these words were too heavy to reconcile with.

Still, the more I thought about the offer, the more I also thought about the promise I made to my mom. I couldn't hate anyone before I met them. I decided to be brave and attend.

I arrived at my friend's house that evening with a backpack—not a normal item to bring to a Thanksgiving dinner. My friend asked, "Why do you have that?"

"Oh, I have an extra shirt and shoes in here." Basketball players often travel with workout gear, because they are frequently heading to or going from a practice or pickup game, so this wasn't way out of the ordinary.

After the customary greetings, we sat down at the table. The tip-off to any Thanksgiving dinner is a prayer, and I wanted no part of that, so I decided to be the broken link in the chain as everyone held hands. It was a painfully awkward moment.

Next came another Thanksgiving ritual—each person took turns saying what he or she was thankful for. When it got to me, I blurted out, "I'm thankful for my religion" so that no one would try to turn me into a Christian. I also expressed gratitude for my health and my family.

But the crown jewel of my cringeworthy experience came when the eating began. As a Muslim, I could eat only halal food. I feared that eating non-halal food—or even touching it—could put me in sin or cause me to lose my religion. I wasn't sure about the status of this meal.

This was the real reason I brought the backpack.

Whenever the group was distracted by conversation and no one was looking, I discreetly dumped the contents of my plate into my backpack, underneath the table. Soon the bag sitting at my feet filled up with a soggy mixture of Thanksgiving dinner items—turkey, stuffing, mashed potatoes, cranberry sauce, and, of course, gravy. Later that night, after dinner, I threw the bag, now leaking gravy, into a dumpster. My first Thanksgiving looked a lot different than the one the Pilgrims had. Now, years later, I look back and laugh. Billy became one of my best friends, and I now eagerly anticipate Thanksgiving—the classic American holiday—every year. I've never told this story to Billy and his family until now!

On another occasion, I was sitting with my teammates after practice. One of them was typing out a Facebook post criticizing President Barack Obama for something I don't remember.

"Dude, what are you doing?!" I exclaimed.

"What happened?" my teammate asked.

"I saw your post."

"And?"

"Well, you know, you might be in jail tomorrow."

"Why?"

"For talking bad about the government."

All my teammates turned around and started to laugh. One of them said, "This is not Turkey, this is America!"

"What do you mean?"

"Well, we have freedom of speech, freedom of religion, freedom of expression. You're not going to be put in jail just because you criticize the government or president."

I couldn't believe what I was hearing. I had never heard this idea of freedom growing up. In Turkey, freedom was something the government chose to give you—or not. The fact that Americans could express their beliefs without being thrown in jail was astonishing.

CHAPTER 4

KENTUCKY BLUES

As my senior year unfolded, I must have had one of the most unusual experiences for a top recruit in history.

Although I was a highly rated prospect, many schools were deterred from recruiting me because I had barely played in high school. Others were nervous that I wouldn't be able to play because of my past payments from Fenerbahçe and my Nike deal. Unlike most top recruits, who get the red-carpet treatment on campus recruiting visits, I didn't tour any schools. I had already decided that I wanted to play for the University of Southern California (I loved the campus and the weather). But USC was banned from playing in the NCAA tournament during the year I would be a freshman, because O. J. Mayo had taken improper benefits before the 2007–8 season. The school didn't want to involve itself in another situation like O.J.'s by taking a risk with me. Additionally, I also planned to be "one and done"—declaring for the NBA draft after one year in school—so I didn't want to miss a chance to play in the tournament. So, in November 2009, I kept my word to Coach Chillious from the University of Washington, who had coached me at the Jordan Brand Classic a year earlier, and signed to play for the Huskies.

With my choice of school now locked in, I kept to a routine over the winter of practicing and playing with Stoneridge, working on my English with friends, and adjusting to life with the Barrys. But in the spring, my college plans changed dramatically. The Nike Hoop Summit is one of the most prestigious tournaments in the world. Every top amateur in the U.S. and the world attends to show off their skills for NBA scouts. Thanks to Max and Tim's connections, I was fortunate enough to be invited to the 2010 Hoop Summit, where I played for the World team against future NBA stars like Kyrie Irving, Harrison Barnes, Tobias Harris, and Brandon Knight. Ironically enough, the facility we played at was the same one that a future team I played for, the Portland Trail Blazers, used. Even though my back was aching that day, I played like a man possessed. I scored 34 points and grabbed 13 rebounds in just 24 minutes, breaking the Hoop Summit scoring record for international players previously held by Dirk Nowitzki, the greatest international player of all time.

After that, college coaches around the country realized that they didn't want to miss out on me. Unfortunately, my old nemesis, Fenerbahçe, was again a thorn in my side. The team—still angry that I had left—began falsely telling American reporters that I had taken $1 million from them. It was true that my family and I had accepted a small salary and money for living expenses from the club, totaling over $100,000, but even that threatened to ruin my eligibility. Reporters and people in the basketball industry began to whisper that I would never be eligible to play college ball because I had forfeited my amateur status. All the coaches lost interest almost immediately.

Except one.

Days after the Hoop Summit, in April, I got a call from John Calipari, one of the greatest coaches of the last several decades. Coach Cal was coaching the Kentucky Wildcats, one of the winningest programs in college basketball history. I was thrilled, not just because Kentucky is the best of the best, but because Calipari had prepared many top talents for the

NBA, including Derrick Rose, Tyreke Evans, John Wall, and DeMarcus Cousins. Calipari also had a reputation for fiercely defending his players whenever their backs were against the wall.

Calipari flew out to California to see me work out at the 24 Hour Fitness gym where Stoneridge Prep practiced. After five minutes of watching me, he told me I had to come play for him. Cal even showed how badly he wanted me by calling one American reporter who was preparing to spread Fenerbahçe's disinformation and convincing him to kill the story. Cal had also fixed a question of eligibility the year before for John Wall, the star point guard who went on to be the No. 1 overall pick in the draft.

Filled with confidence that Calipari would fight for me and prepare my game for the NBA, in April 2010 I decommitted from Washington and signed a letter of intent to play for Kentucky. I was still nervous that I might be ineligible, but Coach Cal reassured me.

"I don't care," Calipari said. "We're going to find a way."

Soon after I signed, I made my first visit to the University of Kentucky campus in Lexington. I'll never forget walking into an empty Rupp Arena, the Wildcats' home court since 1976, where eight NCAA championship banners hang from the rafters. The arena seats 20,000 people, and I had never played in front of a crowd that size. An assistant coach, Orlando Antigua, said, "If we can get you eligible, you will be the king of this court."

"Let's pray it happens."

I mentioned to him how huge the arena was. "Wait until it's full," he said. "Imagine how it would be to play in front of twenty thousand people."

Soon the school year was over and I said my goodbyes to all the Barrys, the family who had put a roof over my head and fed me—had shown me *love*—and never asked for a thing in return. Saying farewell was the saddest moment. My "mom" Kristin cried her eyes out, thinking that I would never contact her again, since I was on the fast track to NBA stardom. As the emotion poured out, I knew that she had come to see me as one of her own sons.

From day one it was clear that Kentucky was not Stoneridge. I had all the food I could eat, and the team supplied me with tons of fresh gear. During my first week on campus, Coach Cal took me out to a restaurant in downtown Lexington. It seemed like every single person on the street knew who I was—and I hadn't even played a game yet! As Cal and I dined, a huge crowd assembled outside, hoping to get autographs or pictures as we exited. Coach was cool to stop and say hello to them, but that was just the tip of the iceberg of the frenzy of Kentucky basketball. "Get used to it," Coach said. "This will be your life from now on."

I arrived earlier than my teammates did to do some summer school, so I didn't meet them until August, at our first team meeting. I sat down next to fellow five-star recruit Brandon Knight, the man who was supposed to carry the team along with me. Coach Cal sternly told us things to do and not do: Don't skip class. Be respectful to professors. And don't bring girls back to the dorm. Immediately after that, a student manager came out with three big posters that resembled wanted posters from the Old West. "These are the girls you must stay away from," he warned, making sure we got a good luck at the three women who were basically stalkers of the basketball players.

The dorm for the basketball players was basically a lodge. I roomed with Josh Harrellson, who, as a senior, was entitled to the very best room. He spent a lot of time with his girlfriend, so I practically had the place all to myself. Josh was really kind, and so were Darius Miller and DeAndre Liggins, two guys who had also been on the team awhile. It was one reason that my teammates truly began to feel like brothers.

A couple of weeks later, I prepared to make my entrance for the University of Kentucky's Big Blue Madness event. Big Blue Madness is like Christmas Day at the University of Kentucky, when thousands of students, fans, and donors come to Rupp Arena to see the players on that year's team make their debut and scrimmage against each other. Each player makes his way into the arena with a special entrance accompanied by flashing lights, booming music, fog machines, and a hyped-up announcer introducing every player. As a kid I had become a huge fan of WWE pro wrestling, and the Undertaker was one of wrestling's biggest stars. My teammates and I got the idea to buy a black, wide-brim hat that looked like the one the Undertaker wore. The fans exploded when I emerged from behind the fake smoke wearing the hat and walking in the Undertaker's slow, deadly serious way, with his theme music blasting. Years later I got to meet the Undertaker, Mark Calaway, at Madison Square Garden and told him how pro wrestling helped me stay sane during my battles with the NCAA.

The Big Blue Madness event indicated to me just how different the college experience in America is compared to everywhere else in the world. I had visited colleges in Turkey, but Kentucky was a world unto itself. I could not believe how big the campus was and how many students there were. At night it gets crazy, and people are partying everywhere (I tried to stay in as much as possible after hearing warnings at our team orientation). When people told me that everything in America would be bigger, flashier, and crazier, I realized that an environment like Kentucky was what they had in mind.

The best part about my one year there was developing deep friendships with my teammates. Because I was so far away from home, I truly regarded them as my family. I was especially close with Terrence Jones and Doron Lamb, and Brandon Knight and Josh Harrellson were great friends too. We certainly bonded on the court, but they taught me so much about life in America as well. They made a lot of effort to help me with schoolwork and explain what Coach Cal was saying in practice. We also loved playing pranks on each other. One day they took me to Firehouse Subs. I didn't know anything about American sandwiches, so they ordered me one loaded with the spiciest ingredients. I had to go to the doctor afterward because it burned my throat, but it was all in good humor.

They also helped me with my English—kinda. Like West Virginia, Kentucky was a hard place to improve my English because there were so many people with thick southern accents. I asked my teammates how I could learn conversational English better, including slang. They all told me that I'd learn a lot of slang and pop culture by watching *Jersey Shore*, the MTV show following a band of wild personalities who spend their summers living at the beach and partying. So, one day I got my dinner, went into my dorm, locked the door, and started concentrating carefully on the show. After watching many episodes, my English did get better, but I laughed to myself thinking, *If this is what America is all about, this country is doomed.*

I also had some outrageous experiences at college parties. I don't drink, so my teammates taught me how to drive so I could be their designated driver. The funny part about all this was that I had never driven a car in my life, and I didn't even have a driver's license—everywhere I went in the U.S. I was usually bumming a ride from teammates, friends, or Max, or taking public transportation. When we managed to make it back to campus despite some close calls on the road, I often had to put them into bed when they had too much to drink.

Throughout college, I always remembered my mom's advice—"Be careful with American girls!"—so I have always tried to follow my religion's teachings when it comes to parties and women. Our coaches were always cautioning us to watch out for girls too, and their warnings were for good reason. One of my teammates was dating a girl whom he later broke up with. A few days later, one of her friends picked him up to give him a ride somewhere. After he got into the car, the girl he had dumped jumped out of the back seat. She and her friend locked him in the car (and I have no idea how this would help convince him to get back together with her). Eventually, his only way to escape was to jump out of a moving vehicle. After that I got very afraid of the girls on campus. I didn't want to mess up my draft status because of a crazy situation like that, so I steered clear of women entirely.

Not long afterward, we had a team meeting about this same girl who was flirting with every member of the team. That had the potential to create disunity among us. We agreed that we had to be united and send her a message to stay away. So, one rainy night at around eleven o'clock, five of us giants—Doron Lamb, Terrence Jones, DeAndre Liggins, Brandon Knight, and I—stuffed ourselves into Brandon's car and drove to her apartment. Our pockets were loaded with packets of ketchup, mayonnaise, mustard, syrup, and other substances useful for vandalism. I'll let you guess what happened next. The next day she called the cops, screaming that the basketball team had desecrated her vehicle.

Coach Calipari called us into his office and asked sternly, "Did you guys do this? Because it's going to be on ESPN if so."

We all denied it.

"Well," Calipari said, "there was a camera in front of the apartment building, and police are reviewing the footage right now."

We all froze and were terrified that we had just caused a huge scandal that would kill our season and draft prospects. But we were saved by an incredible stroke of luck. The police retrieved the footage and began studying it. But right as we got out of the car, a bolt of lightning struck right near the camera. The blast of light destroyed several seconds of footage when we could have been identified.

But we weren't out of the woods yet.

Later that day, one of our assistant coaches confronted us. He knew we had committed the vandalism because he had gotten hold of footage from the security camera outside our dorm. The tape clearly showed us walking out of our dorm with ketchup and mustard packets in our hands. But somehow the assistant coach had gotten the footage deleted immediately—thank you, Coach! Our crew couldn't believe our good fortune and just decided to steer clear of the girl after that.

College, of course, wasn't just all parties and mischief. I took class seriously because my GPA had to be good enough for me to stay on the team, and I had also promised my parents that I would always make education a priority. The good news was that I liked going to class and worked hard with my tutors. The only class I hated was art history—it was a three-hour session right after practice. I was starving. The teacher didn't allow food in class. I dropped it.

One of my favorite classes was history, which gave me an opportunity to learn the story of the country I was living in. I came to understand what the Black community in America had gone through with the legacy of slavery in the U.S. My teammates, most of whom were Black, urged me to pay attention during the lectures to learn things about the civil rights movement I had never heard before. They, of course, were greatly indebted to heroes like Medgar Evers and Martin Luther King Jr., who had sacrificed their lives for the rights of African Americans. Afterward, I would ask them honest questions about race relations in the U.S. and other topics, and they would carefully explain things to me. America wasn't (and still isn't) perfect, but an incredible part of our history is the way that people have fought for their constitutional rights and achieved them. We are truly an inspiration to the world.

Sadly, America's college campuses today are usually not places of free expression and honest dialogue. The purpose of a university is to encourage a free exchange of ideas that can be used for the good of mankind, but most colleges today are fortresses of cancel culture, and social media has only made the problem worse, since people are now terrified of being bullied and shamed online. People with unpopular opinions are routinely intimidated and silenced, and athletes especially are timid to express candid opinions for fear of losing their endorsement deals. I remember one time when I asked my teammates why the n-word was so bad. They were actually happy that I asked in a respectful way so that they could explain that there is no worse word for dehumanizing someone. I don't know if I would get the same response today.

As practice began in the fall, I couldn't wait to hit the court with my new teammates. The Kentucky fans are the most passionate in the country.

We had the best coach and several future NBA players. It was everything I was hoping for after a year being stuck in basketball hell, either not playing or playing against terrible competition.

But as I had learned multiple times before, nothing came easy on my journey to the NBA.

Everyone knew that there were questions about my eligibility because of my history with Nike and Fenerbahçe. As school began, so did the fight with the NCAA—the NCAA announced that they were starting an investigation into my eligibility, and that I could not even practice with the team while it was happening. Fenerbahçe escalated its efforts to try to destroy my career by leaking my payment records to the media and the NCAA—a big *New York Times* story appeared on September 7 reading, "Turkish Team Said It Paid a Top Turkish Recruit." I was irate! Almost immediately the campus became covered with signs and T-shirts proclaiming #FreeEnes. This slogan became the most popular movement in Kentucky history, and even famous UK alums like NBA center DeMarcus Cousins tweeted it.

Looking back, decommitting from the University of Washington might have been a bad decision. The former president of the university, Mark Emmert, was now the head of the NCAA. Maybe staying at his former school would have helped my case. But it was too late now, and I was still happy to be at Kentucky. I knew Coach Cal had my back during the entire process and would fight for me to play.

The first discussion I had with the NCAA over the issue was more like an interrogation. Kentucky's lawyer handling the process prepared me ahead of time, saying, "It's a psychological war. Do not let them put you down. You left millions of dollars to come here and play college basketball. You're gonna play." The lawyer even coached me on what to wear for the meeting. "Don't come in the meeting wearing a watch or any other jewelry. Wear sweatpants. We want them to see you're a college student."

Not long afterward, two very serious, short, middle-aged guys from the NCAA walked into the bland conference room on UK's campus where we had agreed to meet. These men, who could have been former cops, didn't even say hello to me, only grunting "Please sit down" and extending a very official handshake without even bending their elbows. They immediately started saying how hard it was going to be for me to maintain eligibility—a clear pressure tactic. Then they started showing me my financial records from Fenerbahçe and the Nike contract my dad had signed on my behalf. They even had an itemized list of every single piece of gear Nike had ever sent me, down to my socks.

They told me flat out, "You're never going to play basketball in college."

I tried to explain that the Fenerbahçe money was almost totally for expenses, that the Nike contract was signed without my knowledge, and that my dad held on to the cash. I went into deep detail on everything Nike ever sent me, and what I wore and didn't wear. I tried to bargain with them: "I turned down millions to get an education. I'll even sit a year to show you I'm serious."

The whole thing lasted six hours. At the end of it, the NCAA representatives were still firm: "You're not playing."

Kentucky asked for a second meeting. The NCAA agreed, and because I was talking so much about my dad's role in everything, the NCAA wanted to talk to him too, to make sure I was telling the truth.

"My dad is in Turkey."

"Well, we want him here."

It was a huge headache, but I needed to do everything I could to stay eligible. The next day, my dad took a twelve-hour flight from Istanbul to Chicago to sit down with the NCAA. During the meeting, I had to kick him under the table a few times to stop him from nodding off due to jet lag. Fighting through the drowsiness, he admitted to the investigators, "It was my fault, not my son's." Still, after a two- or three-hour meeting, the NCAA insisted, "No, he can't play." We filed an appeal and hoped for the best, especially since Cam Newton, the star quarterback for the Auburn Tigers, had recently won an eligibility battle on similar grounds. If the rules that are in place today at the NCAA had been in place back then,

I'd have played at Kentucky easily and gone on to be the top overall pick in the NBA draft.

Not long after, Coach Cal put it to me straight: "Listen, I'm sorry, but you're not going to play basketball for us ever. The NCAA still hasn't told us yes or no, but I know that you're not going to play."

I couldn't let go of how unfair all this was—from Fenerbahçe sabotaging my career, to the NCAA being so inflexible. The process had played out publicly on ESPN and throughout the sports media, and that also made me embarrassed as a representative of my family, my friends, and the nation of Turkey. Fenerbahçe also kept messaging me on my phone and Facebook, foolishly thinking I'd come crawling back to them after they ruined my shot at playing in college. The head of the Turkish National Basketball Federation, Turgay Demirel, also called me at Fenerbahçe's behest. "Look at Ricky Rubio and Jonas Valanciunas. You can still be like them here." That wasn't good enough for me. I wanted to be in the NBA. And at this point I was so enraged that the basketball powers in Turkey were conspiring to ruin my chances that I would not have returned anyway.

I still wasn't even allowed to practice with the team, so Cal tried to make the best of a bad situation: "If you want, we can make you an assistant coach so you can practice."

"I just want to play basketball, so if I have to be an assistant coach, okay."

Being an assistant gave me some chances to get in the gym to play 1-on-1 against other assistants in private sessions for NBA scouts, but during the games I was on the sideline. Every true basketball player always wants to be on the court, so it was painful to see my teammates battling on the floor while I sat taking notes. Nothing was more frustrating than missing out on valuable playing time and the fun that came from winning alongside my teammates.

On January 7, 2011, after about four months of investigations and appeals, the NCAA made its final ruling that I was permanently ineligible on account of accepting $33,000 more than I should have from Fenerbahçe. When I heard the news, some guys and I were eating lunch and watching ESPN. I was in the back of the room. Then the alert flashed on the screen saying I was done for good. The room got quiet, and everyone turned around and looked at me. All I could do was shrug and mumble a new English phrase I'd learned: "It is what it is."

Later that night I went to the gym all by myself to put up some jumpers and think about my life. It was about 11 p.m., and I was shooting all by myself. Suddenly I saw all my teammates filing into the gym.

"What are you guys doing here?"

"You're our brother. We got you. We're not going to let you go. You're going to go to the NBA anyway."

I've never forgotten how much we felt like a family at that time. They had all showed up late at night to help me forget about my situation for a little while. I almost started crying because I was so moved. We all shared a big team hug. Then we did what we love to do: hoop. We spent a long time playing 5-on-5, letting shots fly, doing show-off dunks, and just having a good time. It wasn't an official team activity, so no one worried about violating any NCAA rules. I don't think my brothers would have heeded them that night anyway.

That midnight run cheered me up for a little while, but I spent the next few weeks in a deep depression. The day after the verdict, the NCAA also ruled that I was still banned from practicing with the team. By this time I hadn't played serious organized basketball in almost two years, when I was still in Turkey. Coach Cal, who was like a father figure to me, sat me down and tried to encourage me: "You're still part of our family. If you want to go back to Europe you can go back to Europe, but if you want to stay here, you can stay here. Just keep getting ready for the NBA."

I was still a Wildcat, but the next several months were some of the hardest and loneliest of my life. From a basketball perspective, nothing had gone right since I came to the States. I had plenty of time to dwell on it all as I spent weeks practicing all by myself. It was just me, shooting, drilling, and conditioning—a terribly lonely experience. The team's strength coach couldn't even legally tell me what to do. He would put pieces of paper on each weight machine with numbers as a hint to me of which exercise to do first, second, third, and so on.

Things outside the gym weren't much better. I liked the campus atmosphere, and had a lot of support from every Wildcats fan, but Kentucky in the middle of winter is not a fun place to be if you grew up in Turkey and spent your first year in the States in Southern California. I cried watching the games because I couldn't be out there helping my teammates, especially since the team went all the way to the Final Four, losing in the National Semifinal game to the eventual champion, the University of Connecticut. I knew that if I had been out there we would have won. To this day, whenever I see Coach Cal, he hugs me and tells me, "I wish you had played for me, son."

I did think about going back to Turkey, but I didn't want to go crawling back to Fenerbahçe. Also, I was projected to be a top pick in the draft in just a few months. I kept thinking about what Max told me: "Keep your eye on the big picture."

If I can just get through this stretch, I told myself, *I'll be okay.*

A few weeks later, on April 7, 2011, I declared for the NBA draft.

CHAPTER 5

THE LEAGUE CALLS

Immediately after the school year ended at the University of Kentucky, I returned to Chicago to get ready for the draft. My friend and trainer Tim Grover again had the responsibility of whipping me into shape. I couldn't have had a better taskmaster—Grover knew all the drills that I would run through at the draft combine (the two-day event when all the prospects show their skills). For two months, Grover ran me through the gauntlet: running, jumping, strength training, defensive slides, bench pressing, shooting, and more. The best part was having a goal to work toward—I could put all my disappointing experiences in high school and college behind me, and focus on the NBA.

On May 17, the NBA held its annual draft lottery. Each year, all the teams that don't make the playoffs are thrown into a literal lottery for the top pick, the winner determined by the selection of a team-branded Ping-Pong ball. The worst teams have more balls in the lottery, giving them a better chance to nab the No. 1 slot. But it doesn't always happen that the team with the worst record gets the first pick.

I watched the lottery at Grover's gym, eager to see which cities I could expect to call my new basketball home. I had already heard scouts and reporters say that I'd probably go in the top five of the draft, but nothing was certain. I hadn't played serious organized basketball in America, and teams that were filled with talent in their frontcourt might not need me. I yearned to go to the Washington Wizards, since D.C. is an international city with a substantial Muslim population and multiple Turkish restaurants. Other than that, I wasn't thrilled about the other teams that would likely pick in the top five. Toronto wasn't in America—the place I came to live my dream. Minnesota was freezing cold. Cleveland was too. But most of all, I didn't want to go to Utah—a state in the middle of nowhere, and not exactly famous for its diversity.

As the top spots rounded into order, my heart sank. Washington nabbed the sixth pick, a spot when I probably wouldn't be available. Toronto then got the fifth pick—good news for me, since I'd probably be gone by then. Cleveland landed the fourth pick. Then Utah got the third, and Minnesota the second. The Los Angeles Clippers won the top spot, but had promised their pick to Cleveland as part of an earlier trade, giving the Cavaliers the No. 1 overall pick. I looked over at Max's face, and he had the same sunken look that I did. I barely touched the Subway sandwich he had brought me for dinner. Grover was more positive, telling me that he was going to attempt to convince a team in a more desirable city to trade up to draft me.

I tried to adopt the best attitude I could as the NBA draft combine started a few weeks later. Lucky for me, it happened to be held that year in Grover's gym, since his reputation as a trainer and his connections throughout the NBA were second to none. Every team was there to evaluate the new crop of players. During the first day, every prospect had his physical qualities measured: running speed, vertical leap, height, hand size, wingspan, and more (including a drug test). I punished the bench press, cranking out rep after rep at 225 pounds in a clear display of the strength that NBA team builders looked for in a center. Afterward, Grover pulled me aside and said, "I'm so proud of you. But this means nothing if you don't kill it tomorrow. No one has seen you play, and they don't know how good you are. You have a lot to prove."

At the end of the first day, the prospects held meetings with teams interested in drafting them. It was like speed dating, with each player going from room to room in a hotel where every team had a room reserved for the talks. Usually a team's coach, assistant coaches, president, general manager, and sometimes the owner would be present. Almost every team wanted me to participate in an interview, but Grover wasn't having it. "It will make no sense for you to meet with them all," he claimed. "You'll be gone before most of them have a chance to pick. We're not going to meet with anyone past the sixth pick."

Grover also drilled in me that every team would ask one crucial question that I must answer correctly: "When they ask you whether you love to win or hate to lose, tell them you hate to lose." I said I would. It probably wasn't the truth at that time, but I would do what he said. "One more thing," he added. "If they ask you who you play like, tell them Moses Malone." This turned out to be a magic answer. I didn't know who Moses Malone was back then, but I later learned he was one of the best NBA players ever, a three-time MVP who retired as the all-time leader in offensive rebounds. Team executives, many of whom were guys who had played or coached against Malone, were impressed when I made this comparison.

The Cleveland Cavaliers were responsible for the strangest thing that happened during these interviews. They must have hired a private investigator to check out my background. At one point they asked me, "On May 15, you took a ride from Chicago back to Kentucky—why did you do that?"

I was stunned that they even knew this mundane detail of my life.

"How do you know that?"

"We're going to invest millions of dollars in one of you. We need to know exactly who you are."

It made sense, but I couldn't stop wondering how they had discovered my whereabouts on that day. There was nothing special about this trip—

I was just going to see friends back on campus—but it was a little spooky to know that Cleveland was monitoring all my movements.

As the second day of the combine started, Grover hyped me up. "Every scout is talking about your numbers from yesterday. But you need to go out and play good ball or it won't mean anything." Fortunately, the day got off to a good start. After shooting drills, I performed well against fellow big men Nikola Vucevic, Tristan Thompson, and Markieff and Marcus Morris. No one could stop me because of my strength and ability to finish over them.

Then things heated up with some 3-on-3. Again Grover came over with his pep talk: "The scouts don't care about any of that. You need to show them that you can play solid team basketball." I can't remember who my teammates were, but they were a very skilled guard and forward. I was cleaning up on the offensive glass, getting easy putbacks.

Then came the 5-on-5—the true test. Grover got in my ear once more: "Nobody cares about three-on-three. If you play like a beast in this five-on-five, you'll be a top-three pick."

At this point I was annoyed at how Tim kept redefining success. "Tim, how can you keep saying it doesn't count?"

He smirked. His motivational tactics had worked.

When the 5-on-5 run started, it was immediately evident that I hadn't played real basketball for two years. My conditioning wasn't the best, and I struggled to catch my breath running up and down the court. The opposing big man scored on me a few times, and my coach called a time-out.

"Are you good?" he asked me. There was no way I was going to say no.

"I'm good, Coach," I responded as I sucked in air.

Grover came up to me as I caught my breath. "This is where they separate good from great. Go out there and focus. Your breathing will come to you. Most of all, have fun!"

That settled me down. The game resumed after the time-out and my teammates began to feed me the ball. I scored in the post a few times and snatched a bunch of boards. During another time-out, I overheard two

GMs asking Grover what he told me during the first break in the action. He told them the truth—that he encouraged me to have fun.

After everyone left for the night and the gym was silent, Tim and I sat and talked for a while. "You played incredibly well. Every GM was asking me about you. They were impressed with your numbers and your performance, especially after you didn't play for two years. But now the real fun starts."

"What do you mean?"

"You're going to go work out for some teams at their facilities. It will feel like pressure. But remember what I told you: have fun and be a good teammate out there."

Over the next month I got calls from almost every one of the teams in the top half of the draft, asking me to visit. Grover refused to let me travel to all those cities—this too would be a waste of time. It would also give the teams an opportunity to show which ones were truly serious about drafting me. "If they really want you, they'll come here to Chicago," Tim theorized.

The first team I worked out for individually was Cleveland. The night I flew in I went to dinner with the coach, Byron Scott, and GM, Chris Grant. They wanted to meet with just me—no Tim, no Max around—just to get a feel for who I was with no advisers present. We had a great conversation about life and basketball . . . until the very end of the meal. In a bizarre turn of events, Chris tried to sell me his car. He told me that he had one that he wasn't driving that much. "If we draft you, do you want to buy it?"

I was completely caught off guard, thinking it might have been a trick question. Was this guy a basketball executive or a used-car salesman? I tried to play it safe.

"If you select me, I'll have to take it for a test drive. And if I like it, I'll buy it." I had a fine workout session with the team the next day, but the car situation left a strange taste in my mouth.

Minnesota was the next team to bring me in for a workout. The first stop on my trip there was the team's practice facility. I am not exaggerating when I tell you that it was inferior to the 24 Hour Fitness gym I practiced at in high school. Nonetheless, I had a solid practice, and thought I had a strong chance to go there.

Then Max shared some eye-popping news with me.

"I don't believe the Timberwolves will select you in the draft. They've already invested significantly in their frontcourt with Nikola Pekovic and Darko Milicic. The general manager has committed substantial financial resources to their contracts, and if they were to draft you, there would likely be pressure from the fan base to give you more playing time than the established centers. This could reflect poorly on the GM's previous financial decisions." As Max explained, "You're young, talented, and already more skilled than both of those players. You have the potential to be the next franchise superstar alongside Ricky Rubio. They could build the entire team around you two. However, this situation demonstrates the political nature of the game." I was also deeply disappointed that I probably would not be going off the board at No. 2 if I didn't go No. 1.

That left Utah—the destination I dreaded going to. At Tim Grover's insistence, their front office and coaching staff came to Chicago to see me work out. Grover also refused to let me play 1-on-1 for them against any players in my draft class. He told the Jazz's delegation, "If you want to play ones against him, go for it."

Some tall old guy I didn't know suited up and prepared to face off against me. "Go out there and destroy him," Tim whispered in my ear.

I banged against this old man for over half an hour, scoring on him at will. On one play, I threw my shoulder into him hard, sending him crashing to the floor with a bang that echoed throughout the empty gym. "You're good," this guy said. "You play ball like we did back in the day."

When we took a break, someone asked me, "You know who that is, right?"

"Nope."

"That's Tyrone Corbin. He used to play in the league. And he's the head coach."

I was mortified that I had laid out the head coach so disrespectfully, and worse, thought I had killed my chances of the Jazz drafting me. But people encouraged me that I had shown the kind of competitive fire that NBA teams were looking for.

A few days later I also worked out for Toronto and the team I desperately wanted to go to: Washington. Their general manager was candid with me about the chance of landing there. The team already had budding young big men in Andray Blatche and JaVale McGee.

"It's between you, Kyrie, and Derrick Williams in the top three picks," the GM said. "If we can convince Utah to trade their pick for ours, plus Andray Blatche, then we'll take you." As it turned out, Utah wanted JaVale, not Andray. Washington didn't want to part with him, so the trade died on the vine.

I prepared to go to either Cleveland or, more likely, Utah. The one silver lining to landing with the Jazz was the chance to play with one of my basketball idols: Mehmet Okur. Mehmet was at that time the most talented Turkish player to ever play in the NBA, even becoming in 2007 the first Turk to ever make an All-Star team. Despite being 6'11", "Memo" was ahead of his time as a big man capable of regularly nailing three-pointers. He passed like a point guard, but could bang in the post if he had to—defying the stereotype that foreign players in the NBA are soft. He had also won an NBA title with the Detroit Pistons in 2004, so he knew what it took to win in the league.

After months of working out and being inundated with rumors, I made a trip home to Turkey in early June, before the draft, to get away from the noise and relax with my family. By this time, Fenerbahçe had stopped harassing me to come back to play for them, but I still felt uncomfortable in my own neighborhood of Kadıköy because of their nutty fans who hated me. And even an ocean couldn't distance me from a new point of stress.

One night I saw the news that the NBA might soon be experiencing a lockout—a dispute between the team owners and the National Basketball Players Association that would mean the immediate stoppage of all league business on July 1, days after the draft. That meant no communication between teams and players, no practices, and—most critically—no paychecks (Believe it or not, many NBA players live check to check.) This battle between millionaires and billionaires over money would eventually drag on for months. For many it meant financial hardship. But it gave other players opportunities to showcase their skills in nontraditional ways: Kevin Durant, for example, exploded for 66 points in a game at New York City's legendary Rucker Park. Spurs point guard Tony Parker played for a French team for less than $2,000 per month—pennies by NBA standards—just to stay sharp and gain exposure for that squad.

I wasn't in the NBA yet, but I also benefited from the lockout. One day in early June, Grover called me. "This might be the best thing that ever happened to you!" he declared.

I was perplexed. "Why is that?"

"Every good player will pull their name out of the draft if they think the lockout will last a long time. So, your chances of being top three—or maybe the top pick—will go up."

Just as Tim predicted, top players like Jared Sullinger and Harrison Barnes soon withdrew from the draft. That was great for me, but I began to wonder about how a lockout would affect the beginning of my career.

In the meantime, my family was overjoyed at how my life was about to change, and helped prepare me accordingly. They wanted me to shine on draft night, and my siblings each chipped in to make sure I presented myself well. My sister Betül acted as my stylist, helping me pick out my suit, tie, and shirt combination. My brother Kerem coached me on my walk to the stage, handshake, and hat modeling. And my little brother Ahmet pretended to be a reporter, lobbing the questions I would likely be asked. I didn't realize at the time how precious this fun family moment was, years before our time together in person would be cut off permanently because of the Turkish government's political persecution.

I returned to the U.S. days before the draft with my father and my brother Kerem. On the morning of the big day, June 23, 2011, I went downstairs to have breakfast at the hotel in Manhattan where we were staying. In the dining room sat a lonely and stressed Brandon Knight, one of my teammates at Kentucky forecasted to go in the top ten. Brandon did not have a great experience during the draft process—scouts didn't love his game as much as he thought they would. He thought he had a chance to go third, because the Jazz really needed a point guard. But if he didn't, there was a strong chance he would drop. I tried to console him. "The Jazz are either going to pick me or you."

He sighed. "Yeah."

"I hope it's you."

"What do you mean?"

"You're my brother, and I want the best for you."

Brandon started fighting back tears. The competitiveness of pro sports has a sad way of sometimes splitting friends apart. We'd spent a precious year of our basketball journey together in college and made a lot of memories as Wildcats on campus. Through all the madness of big-time college hoops and the roller coaster of the NBA draft, we were both thankful that our bond as basketball brothers was stronger than any desire to surpass one another in draft status.

The wait for the evening to begin was torture, even more so because my suit was late to arrive at the hotel that day, putting me on edge. When it finally arrived, I put on my new threads and boarded the bus that would transport all the players from the hotel to the draft venue: the Prudential Center in Newark, New Jersey, normally the home of the then–New Jersey Nets.

Every likely top draftee is given a table on the floor of the arena in front of the stage at the draft and is allowed to fill it up with friends and family. Surrounding me were my dad, my brother, Coach Calipari, my agent Max, and Tim Grover. My dad could sense my nervousness as my knees shook and I sweated through my brand-new suit, custom-made for this occasion. He tried to calm me down, saying, "Trust God. You did everything you could."

Being seated at the table in front of thousands of fans, reporters, and team personnel only amped up the pressure of what was about to unfold. At the front of the arena was a stage with a giant draft board hanging above it to track who each team picked. Lights flickered and cameras popped to capture the tense faces of the new crop of NBA stars. Additionally, every top prospect was seated near each other, so we could all size one another up to see each other's nervousness (or confidence). Not far away, an ESPN crew chattered away, dissecting each player's strengths and weaknesses. On Twitter, reporters posted rumors of who they heard would be picked and where, up until the last second before the action started. It was a sensory overload of the highest order.

As the draft commenced, NBA commissioner David Stern—a man who did a great job taking the NBA global—strode to the podium and announced the first pick: Kyrie Irving. It was a great choice by Cleveland, since Kyrie went on to become the Rookie of the Year, an NBA champion in 2016, and an eight-time All-Star, as of this writing. Kyrie certainly deserved to go No. 1 overall, but I couldn't help but be mad at the NCAA at the instant Commissioner Stern called his name. I knew I could have been the top pick if I had been allowed to showcase my skills in college.

I continued to wait nervously for the next pick, knowing that no matter what happened, I was still poised to make history as the highest-drafted Turkish player ever. After another eternity, Stern took the stage again and announced that the Minnesota Timberwolves had taken Derrick Williams. I wasn't surprised at this pick. Still, I was bummed.

Then the Utah Jazz went on the clock. I wasn't sure if they would grab me. The team needed a point guard and already had some promising big men on their roster. Many top prospects have been humiliated on draft day by sliding far past the point they expected to be picked, eventually sitting all alone in the greenroom. I shuddered at the thought of the cameras fixating on me, isolated, as the guy teams didn't want.

Stern made the journey back to the microphone. My heart was pounding so hard I was afraid it would crack my sternum. Then I heard the news I'd been working for almost a decade to hear:

"With the third pick in the 2011 NBA draft, the Utah Jazz select Enes Kanter from Istanbul, Turkey, and the University of Kentucky."

My heart, which had been beating at warp speed, suddenly slammed to a halt. As the cameras clicked and the fans burst into applause, every frustration of the past two years instantly melted away in the excitement of this moment of pure bliss. I stood up and hugged my dad, who whispered in my ear, "I told you to trust God. I'm so proud of you." I also shared hugs with the guys who had been my greatest basketball mentors: Calipari, Grover, and Max. *I finally have a team!* I thought happily. I had hated the idea of going to Utah in the lead-up to the draft, but now I couldn't wait to get there.

I proceeded onto the stage to shake the commissioner's hand and put on a Jazz hat. I walked carefully, remembering advice my brother Kerem had told me weeks before: "Walk straight, don't trip, and put your hat on with two hands!" I looked out into the audience and saw some fans waving Turkish flags. I couldn't wait to make them proud.

After greeting the commissioner and putting my hat on, the commissioner quietly asked me, "How is Dr. Kanter doing?" It was nice of him to ask about my father, but all I could muster was, "He's doing really well. Thank you for this opportunity."

Moments later, after leaving the stage, I sat for my first-ever interview, carefully articulating the answers I'd rehearsed with Ahmet. I dedicated my rookie season to the Kentucky Wildcat fans and promised that I would bring scoring, rebounding, and tough post play to the team. Then came phone calls from the Jazz's team leaders, each of them thrilled to have me as a cornerstone of the franchise's future. My mom was delighted that I'd landed in Utah. In her view, Salt Lake City was "the holiest place in America," since about 50 percent of the city is part of the Church of Jesus Christ of Latter-day Saints. Mormons don't drink or do drugs, so she was happy that those temptations would be minimal.

That night, I went with my family to a nearby restaurant to celebrate.

Suddenly I spied across the dining room my old on-court rival: Jonas Valanciunas, whom the Toronto Raptors had taken two spots behind me. We approached each other and shared a big hug. With his agent acting as his interpreter, Jonas told me, "We've been battling each other since we were sixteen. Look at us now."

"It's not over," I joked with him. "I'll see you in the league."

The next day Max and I took a flight to Utah so that I could meet with the front-office personnel, see the team's facility, and do a photo shoot. As I toured the facility, I encountered my basketball hero, Mehmet Okur, lifting weights. Memo gave me a bear hug and offered to take me to lunch that afternoon, an offer I was overjoyed to accept. Soon I was sitting in the passenger seat of Mehmet's red Ferrari, absorbing his advice on making it as an NBA player: "This life is just starting for you. You might not start in the first game, but if you keep working, you'll get to be a starter. It's a long season, and you'll have good games and bad ones. Stay positive, and be a good locker room guy, because this team will be your family." I took his words to heart, waiting for my first opportunities to bond with my new teammates.

But, as it turned out, I had to wait much longer than I hoped.

A little over a week after the draft, the world learned the news that the NBA owners and players could not reach a new labor agreement. As a result, there was now a lockout. The season would not start until the deadlock was broken, and no one knew how long that would be. Until it lifted, players could not interact with their teams whatsoever.

The day the news broke I stayed in bed all day in a deep depression. *My luck is so terrible*, I thought. *No high school, no college, and now no NBA. I may never play basketball again. I hope this is just a test from God.* By God's grace, I eventually got myself out of bed and convinced myself I would get through it.

Persevering meant continuing to work on my game, as Coach Corbin had urged me to do on the phone the day before the lockout. I relocated to Los Angeles for the next couple of months, playing pickup games with other pros around town. To help pay the bills before my first NBA check came in, I also played in an exhibition game at Rupp Arena in Lexington against other NBA players—ironically, the only time I ever played in an organized game on Kentucky's home floor. Most memorable about this game was the tough chore of guarding Zach Randolph, a 6'9", 250-pound bruiser who punished anyone who dared to bang with him in the post. Zach, who had been in the league since 2001, completely destroyed me with his enormous size and rough play. *I have work to do*, I thought.

When I returned home that summer, the embarrassment of all that had happened with my college career felt long gone. I was treated to an incredible hero's welcome in Turkey when I made my first trip back after being drafted. Hundreds of people waited in the airport just to get a glimpse of me. When I got off the plane, they threw flowers around my neck and grabbed me for picture after picture. It felt so special to be beloved by my countrymen. But oh how things would change in the years to come!

I also honed my abilities by playing for the Turkish national team in the 2011 European championships. It was always important to me to wear the Turkish flag on my chest, and I regretted that I couldn't play in 2010, but I was mad at how the Turkish National Basketball Federation had sided with Fenerbahçe in the battle over my future, and I was also busy getting ready to play for Kentucky. Now, in 2011, I was ready to play.

Shortly before the tournament began, the team fired us up by introducing us to Erdoğan, who was then the prime minister. They took us to a former Ottoman palace in Istanbul and brought us into a room where we lined up to meet him. He arrived and shook everyone's hand one by one. Then we sat down with him for his "pep talk." I didn't really pay attention at all—I wasn't into anything political back then—but I know he was droning on with propaganda. I mostly played with my phone under the table. All I really remember was Hedo Türkoğlu, an NBA star, asking him for more money for playing in the tournament.

I guess Erdoğan's speech didn't fire us up enough, because the national team didn't advance past the second round of the 2011 tournament, but I gained priceless experience playing in the tournament in Lithuania against skilled NBA big men like Marc and Pau Gasol, Dirk Nowitzki, Chris Kaman, and of course Jonas Valanciunas. Hedo served as a mentor to me throughout the tournament, hyping me up and explaining to me different strategies. Later, politics would split me apart from my basketball big brother.

After returning to the U.S. one morning in December I woke up to our team's player representative to the NBA players union, Raja Bell, telling me the lockout was over. I immediately traveled back to Utah for a hastily assembled training camp before a shortened season. I decided to choose 0 for my jersey number. Not only did it remind me to stay humble, but it also poked fun at my "one-and-done" experience at Kentucky. I was maybe the first player in NCAA history to go zero-and-done.

I was thrilled to finally be with the team, but I couldn't dodge an obvious question: Where would my playing time come from? The 2011–12 Utah Jazz were loaded with big men who could play. Al Jefferson was a true center who had been second on the team in scoring the previous year. Derrick Favors—like me, a former No. 33 overall pick—was a young, explosive power forward and center still looking to prove himself as a force in the league. Paul Millsap wasn't drafted high but was a tireless rebounder who never took plays off. Okur was also in the mix. Many top picks are automatically given plenty of playing time, but mine would have to be earned the hard way. I was used to destroying the competition in high school with ease. Now I was going up against the best players in the world—grown men who fought every day to keep their place in the league. Being drafted high didn't mean anything—I had everything to lose, and even more to prove. I took confidence from knowing that people who built basketball teams for a living thought that I belonged with the best.

To their credit, the Jazz worked to solve the big-man logjam, but the way they did it was painful. On December 22 the Jazz shipped Okur off to the New Jersey Nets. I was heartbroken, because I had looked forward to playing with a man I considered a big brother and mentor. But the team's management reassured me and Derrick Favors, saying, "We traded Okur so you two can get minutes and develop." Derrick became a frequent matchup in practice and we loved going hard against each other, envisioning ourselves becoming the frontcourt duo that would one day lead Utah to its first title.

In Mehmet's absence, Al Jefferson became my true mentor during my first year. He had come into the league right out of high school and was still just twenty-six years old despite being in the league for seven years. He had accumulated a lot of knowledge in that time, and I was grateful for his willingness to share it with me. He and I had a similar game as classic, back-to-the-basket big men. Through countless games of 1-on-1 after practice, Al showed me a ton about footwork, scoring moves in the post, and little tricks to get calls from the referees. I'll always be grateful to him for how he helped me find my way in the best basketball league in the world.

The NBA released the regular season schedule a few weeks before the season started. For days I refused to look at it. I had no desire to get agitated over which team would be our opponent in my first game and which players I might have to face. Eventually I summoned the courage. The first game would be on December 27, 2011, a road game against the Los Angeles Lakers. To play the Lakers as a rookie was like a young boxer going up against Muhammad Ali in his first professional fight. The Lakers were stacked with stars who had won two championships together, led by Pau Gasol, Andrew Bynum, Metta World Peace (formerly known as Ron Artest), Derek Fisher, and, of course, the unstoppable Kobe Bryant.

Although Kobe held godlike status in my mind, I had actually been fortunate to meet him on one of my trips home to Turkey that past summer. Kobe was part of a Nike trip to Europe at the same time, and Nike brought us together as the head coaches of two youth teams facing off in an exhibition game. Kobe and I took a picture after the game, and he gave me some brief advice for succeeding in the NBA. True to his mentality, which was unrivaled in intensity, he bluntly told me, "Every detail counts. If you don't commit yourself one hundred percent, don't even bother. Take care of your body. Eat well. Sleep well. You can't party at night and play effectively the next day." His encouragement helped shape my approach to being a professional.

Six months later, Kobe carried this same intensity in the pregame warmups, a champion ready to slay whoever stood in his way in his quest for his next title. I remember standing for the national anthem and feeling my knees tremble with nerves, preparing to compete against the same man I used to watch on TV while sneaking into the living room in the middle of the night. I was finally living my dream—but was terrified at how it was beginning! Playing in the Staples Center in front of 20,000 screaming Lakers fans is a brutal way to begin your career—especially when you haven't played a real game of organized ball in two and a half years.

Late in the first quarter, Coach Corbin substituted me into the game. As I waited at the scorer's table to check in for the first time, Kobe also got set at the table to return to the game after taking an early breather.

"What's up, Enes?" he asked.

Kobe and I had already met a few months ago, but I was still starstruck, like a teenage girl swooning over the Beatles. *Oh my God, Kobe knows me!* I gasped to myself. That was my true "welcome to the NBA" moment.

More than anything during my first game, I was mesmerized by watching the same Kobe Bryant I had admired as a kid take control of the game. At the end of the night, my stat line for that game was mixed: I shot only 1-for-7 from the field, but I did manage to score 5 points and grab 11 rebounds in 20 minutes. More than anything, I was disappointed that we lost 96–71.

Of course, I had a couple of classic rookie moments. Near the end of the first quarter, I grabbed an offensive rebound and went up for a shot under the basket before getting clubbed by a defender.

The referee blew the whistle. "Foul!" he cried. "Two shots!"

These would be my first-ever free throws in the NBA. Coach Corbin took a quick, thirty-second time-out before I went to the free-throw line, probably to help me calm down. I don't remember a word he said during the break. All I thought about was being on the line alone in front of the maniac Laker fans and the Black Mamba: Kobe.

I stepped to the stripe with my legs quaking. Behind the net, the fans were trying to distract me, waving inflatable thundersticks and making an avalanche of noise. I spun the ball backward to get in my preshot groove, my hands trembling uncontrollably. All the while, Kobe was talking trash at me. I have no recollection of what he was saying, but I am sure it was too profane to repeat it here even if I did remember.

Forgetting to pray beforehand, I let my first shot go.

Brick.

The crowd delighted in my failure. My teammates slapped my hands for encouragement. Kobe kept talking.

Then, before the second attempt, I quietly prayed, *Bismillah—in the name of God—don't let me miss this one!*

I squared up, flicked my wrist, and let it go.

Good! My first-ever point!

I jogged back to our end of the court. *I better get used to all this,* I thought.

Now on defense, I began to guard Pau Gasol under the rim. Pau is one of the most skilled and cunning offensive big men ever, so I was completely focused on him. On the other side of the court, Kobe had the ball. He faked out his defender, Raja Bell, with a jab step, giving himself a clear path to the rim. Everyone knew what happened when Kobe had room to take flight—he was going to rain down fire on anyone foolish enough to challenge him in the air.

Of course, as the big man protecting the rim, that was my job.

The coaches yelled at me to leave Pau and go help against Kobe. I saw the whole scene unfolding as if I were watching from the sidelines—I was about to be a victim of a violent Kobe slam in my first NBA game.

I had a split-second decision to make: stay at home on Pau or go confront Kobe.

Coach Tyrone Corbin was still screaming: "Help on Kobe, Enes!"

It wasn't a hard choice.

Kobe took one dribble and gathered his body to launch into the stratosphere. I decided, *I can't be his prey on ESPN's Top 10 highlights in my first game. There's no way.*

Kobe ripped down a thunderous jam untouched, and the crowd exploded. So did my coach—furious with me for not playing the proper defense.

Sorry, Coach. I couldn't let Kobe put me on *SportsCenter* in my first game.

Afterward, Corbin was willing to let it slide. "I know you didn't want to get posterized in your first game. It's okay. But next time I'm not going to be so nice."

CHAPTER 6

BIRTH OF AN ACTIVIST

Prior to being drafted, I dreaded going to Utah. Salt Lake City was in the middle of nowhere, far away from the cosmopolitan cities where I felt more comfortable. But because I'm a simple guy, and a Muslim who strives to live according to my faith, including not drinking, the center of the Mormon universe was ironically the best city in America for me to land. A lot of players who begin their NBA careers in party spots like Los Angeles or Miami wash out in a few years, but here there weren't a lot of distractions off the court—just Mormon missionaries knocking on my door, with whom I had intelligent exchanges on religious views. I was scared that everyone I would encounter there would try to convert me, but almost everyone was respectful of my faith.

Additionally, the Utah fans were incredible. Back then, the Jazz were Salt Lake's only major professional sports team (other than the Real Salt Lake soccer team), so the team absorbed almost all the city's sports attention. As a result, the fans were (and still are) among the most passionate in the league for decades, going back to when John Stockton was running the pick-and-roll with Karl Malone in the 1990s or when Adrian Dantley was lighting it up in the 1980s. I loved playing in front of them.

My salary in my first season was more than $4 million. But I didn't see nearly that much after taxes, a fact that shocked me the first time I checked my bank account after signing my contract. NBA players must pay taxes to every state they play in, and being in the Western Conference meant lots of trips to high-tax California. Add in federal taxes and agent fees, and most players see much less than the top-line number.

Even though I was earning big bucks, I didn't let NBA money lead me to a high-spending NBA lifestyle. Before the draft, everyone wanted to know what kind of car I was going to buy. Once I got to Utah, I leased one, and lived in a rented house. For food I stuck to what I loved most: halal fast food. My pregame meal was a cheeseburger and fries, and I often ate popcorn before the games too. But over time I had to adjust my diet, after realizing I was becoming much too sluggish before tip-off.

In gratitude for their help in achieving my dreams, I sent the balance of my first NBA check to my family, telling them, "If you didn't help me, if you didn't encourage me to go to America, none of this would have happened." The next day, they sent it right back. They said, "This is your life now. You earned this."

On the court, Al Jefferson schooled me on the nuances of different players around the league. In one of the first games I ever played, against the San Antonio Spurs, I was matched up on Tim Duncan, an eventual five-time champ whom many regard as the best power forward of all time. Tim is a nice guy, but I couldn't believe how friendly he was to me during the game, when you're supposed to be at war with your opponent. While most players talk trash to rookies, Tim asked me, "How's Utah? How's your family?"

I told Al during a time-out, "He's so nice to me. I want to play him every game!"

Al just shook his head. "No, man! That's his trick to soften you up! Look how many points he has!"

It was true. Duncan was on his way to 30 points, if I remember correctly. He was a master psychologist in making you like him so that you played a little less hard against him. Then he dominated you. In that first game against Tim, Coach Corbin saw how my intensity was dropping, the more friendly I became with him. He pulled me from the game while dishing out a brutal scolding over my naive attitude.

As my first season went on, I became increasingly comfortable with my new teammates. After about the twentieth game of the season, I was sitting in the front of the team plane with Paul Millsap, Al Jefferson, Jamaal Tinsley, and Devin Harris, all NBA veterans. Al asked me, "How do you think things are going so far?"

I spoke the truth: "Everything is amazing! I don't even feel like a rookie."

Al and the guys all broke into mischievous smiles. "Oh, it's on now!" Al exclaimed. I had no idea what he meant.

My fellow rookie Alec Burks overheard the conversation. He ran up to the front of the plane and begged me to shut my mouth. "You're going to regret this," he stated.

I soon found out why.

Prior to this moment, I was not initiated into the long-established NBA ritual of rookie hazing. Soon everything changed. Before the next flight, my veteran teammates showed up with a pink Barbie backpack. "You have to carry this around on every road trip," they said. "If you forget it, you're going to pay the price." For the next few months, the world was treated to the sight of a 6'11" man lugging around a Barbie backpack everywhere he went.

But that was far from the worst hazing I endured. I had to carry the team's luggage from the bus to the plane and back. Buckets of ice water were thrown on me in the shower. My phone and clothes were routinely hidden in the locker room, and I had to ask the clubhouse attendant to tell me where the guys stashed them. My teammates even forced me to serve food and drinks on the team plane, basically making me the team flight attendant. Guys would push the button above their seat to demand that I cater to their every need. It was not the thing I wanted to do at 1 or 2 a.m. after playing a basketball game.

The most maddening duty was bringing the team donuts every morning, even during road games. Gordon Hayward made me sign a contract saying I would do this or else pay a $500 fine to him each time I forgot! At home, fulfilling this obligation was mostly not a problem—I simply had to swing by the donut shop on the way to practice. But it was much harder on the road. In the days before DoorDash or Uber Eats, I had to wake up early, identify a donut shop, and hail a cab there. It was exhausting! I thought the abuse would subside after my rookie year, but when there proved to be no rookies on our roster during our second year, I had to endure all this again! Fortunately, my teammates appreciated all I did for them, and they bought me a Gucci wallet at the end of my second year in exchange for putting up with all the teasing.

For entertainment, my teammates loved to go out to bars and clubs, but I had no idea how they played the next day after partying all night. I sometimes went out with them, just to hang out, but it really wasn't my preferred scene. Otherwise, our team bonding activities were good. When our team went to the Dr. Martin Luther King Jr. Museum in Memphis, I was shocked to learn that Black people were once forced to sit in the back of the bus and drink from a separate fountain.

Before the beginning of my second year, the NBA held its yearly rookie transition program. The program didn't happen before my first year because of the lockout, so I and the other guys from my draft class participated. It was there that I heard skin-crawling stories from former players of behaviors to avoid. Chris Herren, for example, was a former guard for the Boston Celtics who had ruined his life with heroin. Herren described how his descent started with the OxyContin, Vicodin, and Percocet he took during his playing days. Denver Nuggets forward Kenneth Faried and many other guys were crying as Chris told his sad tale of losing his NBA dream to drugs. I'm happy to say he's now been sober since 2008 and has built an incredible career as an addiction counselor and motivational speaker.

The lecture that made the biggest impression on me came from Antoine Walker, a former All-Star forward for the Boston Celtics. Antoine told us how he had squandered $108 million in career earnings, eventually having to file for bankruptcy in 2010, just two years after he retired from the NBA. His great warning—besides not overspending on houses, cars, and jewelry—was to be careful who you associate with. "People you barely know are going to try and become your best friends," he cautioned. "But they don't see you as anything but a dollar sign. The hardest thing in the world is to tell people no. Be smart with your money. Once you're retired, you're going to think the money will keep coming in. It won't." Between wild spending habits, high taxes, divorces, and failed business ventures, it's not surprising that about 60 percent of NBA players are broke within five years of retiring from the league, as the National Basketball Players Association has publicly disclosed.[1]

Off the court, I continued to have a few embarrassing moments. Sometime during my first few years in the league, I had become friends with a girl whom I met at a charity event. She was extremely kind to me in assisting me with my English. One day before my third year, she invited me to dinner at her family's house. I suggested Wednesday. She told me Friday was best.

"Why Friday?"

"Well, that's when we do Shabbat."

"What's Shabbat?"

"Shabbat is when we come together on Friday night and break bread together and pray."

"Pray? What do you mean?"

"Yeah, pray. That's what Jewish people do."

I couldn't believe that I'd been friends with one for more than a year.

If I had known about her identity from the beginning, I would have never even talked to her. *This is too much*, I told myself. *I can't be friends with this person.* I then blocked her from my phone.

But the next day, I again remembered what my mom had told me years ago. I couldn't shut out a friend who had already demonstrated so much kindness. My mind filled with fear that my friend and her family would try to convert me at their dinner, but I resolved to give it a chance. I called her back.

"I'll come, but I'm only going to stay there for thirty minutes. I'm not gonna pray with you guys. I'm not gonna drink alcohol. And I'm not gonna eat pork."

She said, "Good, because we don't eat pork either."

"Okay," I replied. "And one last thing: I want you to write all this down so there's no misunderstanding."

"Okay, deal."

That Friday afternoon, right before going to her house, I called a friend of mine living in America. I told him, "Listen, I'm going to my friend's house."

"Okay, so why are you calling me?"

"Well, because she's Jewish."

He started to yell at me.

"You're crazy! What are you doing? What is wrong with you?" They are going to eat babies and drink blood. Have fun I guess!"

I told him, "I called you to warn you. If you don't hear from me after the next two hours, you better call the police." I gave him the address I was going to.

"Okay, man. You're a good Muslim, and you don't have to do this. But if you do, be careful!"

When I arrived at my friend's house, she came outside to welcome me in. As we entered the doorway to go inside, she tapped an emblem hanging near the entrance and then kissed her hands.

"What are you doing, you weirdo?" I asked her.

"That's a *mezuzah*."

"Why did you do that?"

"Because it's like a prayer, it protects us."

I thought to myself how interesting this was, because many Muslims have a similar ritual for entering homes.

Walking into her parents' home, I received a warm welcome from my friend's mother. Because she knew I was Turkish, she had gotten me a box of Turkish delight—the best kind available in America. This gesture also provoked a lot of thinking—it was not the kindness I expected from a group of Jewish Americans.

The conversation at the dinner table was also friendly. Her mom and dad endlessly sung praises about Turkey, which they had visited. "It's such a peaceful and beautiful country. We want to go back!" I didn't understand how, as Jews, they could embrace Turkey and Muslims so heartily.

Then I began to panic. I had intended to pull the same stunt with my backpack that I did on Thanksgiving. But I forgot to bring it. I started thinking about how I could escape from this predicament without eating the food. I was extra wary of eating their Jewish kosher cuisine—it could be poisoned! But after her dad prayed over the meal and started to break the bread, I said to myself, *Screw it. I can't live like this.*

At first I was uneasy while eating, carefully tasting every bite before swallowing. But soon I became comfortable. It helped that I realized how many traditional Jewish foods aren't that different from traditional Turkish ones. To this day, I remember the bread being some of the tastiest I've ever had in my life. When it was time for the wine to be poured, they gave me grape juice. "We know you're Muslim and don't drink," they said. It was a thoughtful gesture, but I still had my suspicions, so I smelled the grape juice before I drank it to verify that it wasn't wine. This hospitality was the exact opposite of everything I expected from a Jewish family.

Overall, it was the best night I had had to that point since I left Turkey. Most remarkable were the similarities between many of their religious traditions and Islamic ones. The songs, dances, and washing of hands are found in both cultures. When I told them at the end of the night that I'd love to come back again, they said, "You're welcome anytime you want! Don't wait for Shabbat!"

On the way home, I called my friend and told him, "Listen, man. I had the best night ever!"

He wasn't convinced. "Wait until you go back to your place—the poison might kick in!"

"If that's the case, then oh well."

Later that night, sitting quietly in my room, I became very emotional. I was angry with people who had brainwashed me during my childhood, before I became involved with the Hizmet community. I kept thinking of the millions of kids in the Middle East growing up harboring anti-Semitic, anti-West, anti-American attitudes, just because of politicians' hate speeches, and who would grow up hating Jews without ever even meeting one. Until a few hours ago, I had been just like them. I began to feel that somehow, someday I had to use my life to put a stop to that ignorance. It was on me to show the world that we are all brothers and sisters. Soon after this, I bought a Bible and a Book of Mormon and looked up the Torah online. I started studying and comparing them with the Quran. The wheels were starting to turn.

=

My first year ended uneventfully. We made the playoffs in 2012, but the Spurs defeated us 4–0 in the first round. It was frustrating getting inconsistent playing time throughout the season, but I showed enough improvement to deserve more for next season. In the offseason, the Jazz sent me and Derrick Favors down to Louisiana, where Jazz legend Karl Malone lived on a gigantic backwoods ranch. The team's goal was to have "the Mailman" teach us new moves and drill good conditioning techniques into us. But that wasn't all we did. Karl is a major hunter, whose home was stuffed with mounted heads of exotic animals he had shot all over the world: lions and bears and other beasts. After one workout, Karl asked me, "Have you ever shot a gun before?" I replied that I hadn't.

"Do you want to try?" he asked.

"Not really," I admitted.

Karl didn't care. We went out in an open space and shot some cans. It was my introduction to America's Second Amendment right to bear arms—something that is completely foreign to most people around the world. It was fun shooting, but I didn't have a big appetite to make it a hobby. Later, Karl and I rode back to his house in a golf cart that I was driving. I swerved to avoid hitting a pothole and tipped over the cart—an extremely dangerous situation. Either of us could have been killed, but we survived. Most impressive was that Karl got up like nothing had happened and single-handedly lifted the eight-hundred-pound golf cart off its side like he was Hercules. Even at almost fifty years old, he still had mind-blowing strength.

My second year saw increases in my points per game and minutes per game, and I had lots of fun with my teammates on and off the court, even despite the continued hazing. My career was looking promising, especially after a 23-point, 22-rebound game against Charlotte on March 1. I also had a moment of enlightenment about what it would take to endure in the league. In one game against Kevin Garnett and the Boston Celtics, I saw how Garnett brought a maniacal intensity to cheering for his team, trash talking, and competing. On one play he made a fadeaway jumper over me as I hit his forearm. He screamed *"And one!"* in my face like no player had ever done before. Seeing Garnett's relentless desire to win helped transform my mentality and fired me up to hate losing.

The only major downside to my second year was an excruciating separated shoulder I suffered ten games before the end of the year. Hamed Haddadi, a massive center from Iran, collapsed on top of it as we were scrambling for a loose ball. The break was so bad that some bone was sticking out from the skin. I was in total agony and underwent surgery in Chicago a few days later. I wrote "Bismillah" on a piece of paper before the operation and gave it to the surgeon. The injury put me out of commission for six months, meaning I'd miss the 2013 European championships. But the upside to the injury was that the head of the Turkish cultural center came to visit me in Chicago—a very kind gesture. We soon became friends, and he served as a gateway to many new Turkish friends in the U.S.

It was through this connection that I eventually got to know Fethullah Gülen himself. Gülen was a highly influential Turkish Islamic scholar who preached a philosophy of tolerance and moderation. Even though I had attended Hizmet schools during my youth, my real exposure to his ideas and beliefs happened after I met him in the U.S. My unfounded bias against others have been completely transformed after this. I realized I was completely wrong in my earlier ideas that were shaped by the toxic environment in eastern Turkey. At this time, Gülen had been living in Pennsylvania since 1999, and later in the year, after the surgery, I traveled to meet with him in person for the first time, not long before a corruption scandal erupted in Turkey.

When I walked into the room in which he was sitting alone, he raised his head and invited me to sit down. He looked very deep into my eyes and asked me, "Do you play soccer or volleyball?"

I smirked and replied, "Neither one. I play basketball."

It didn't bother me that Gülen didn't know who I was. Basketball wasn't that popular a sport in Turkey—soccer reigns supreme in the country, although it did become a little more famous when Turkey hosted the FIBA world championship in 2010 and the national team made it all the way to the finals, which we lost against the U.S. I later found out that as my stature as a famous Turkish athlete continued to grow, Gülen watched parts of my games and some of my highlights.

Over the course of our conversation, I saw that he was genuine in upholding the beliefs that were taught in the Hizmet schools. "It doesn't matter what your background, skin color, ethnicity, or religion, are," he emphasized. "We must leave our differences behind and see what we have in common. We need to make this world better together." I completely agreed—and being exposed to America's traditions of tolerance had deepened my beliefs that people are capable of uniting at a national level despite their differences.

Over the next several years, Gülen and I became great friends. In Turkey, Erdoğan has the nickname of "the tall man" because of his 6'1" frame (believe it or not, that is actually taller than the height of the average Turkish man). One day after Gülen and I prayed together, he turned around and joked, "You're the real tall man." We became such good friends that Gülen himself took to calling me his "spiritual son." He often expressed how he wanted to come watch me play, but his poor health situation prevented it. Nevertheless, it was such a blessing to learn directly from him about the importance of coexistence, freedom, democracy, and justice all around the world.

I spent the summer after my second year visiting my family in Turkey. I was glad to be home, but I could also see how the Erdoğan regime was trending in an authoritarian direction and escalating poisonous rhetoric. In early 2013, Erdoğan compared a rival Turkish political party to Syrian dictator Bashar al-Assad's Baath Party—the implication being that it hates its own people.[2] In May 2013, protests in Istanbul's Gezi Park over an urban redevelopment plan exploded into nationwide demonstrations against the erosion of secularism and freedom of expression. It was the greatest challenge to Erdoğan's rule that he had faced over the course of his decade in power. The police responded with force in many instances, leaving 22 people killed and more than 8,000 injured across the country. A police dragnet expanded across the country targeting anyone remotely linked to the nationwide protest movement. Even hotel owners in Istanbul who aided injured, fleeing protesters were labeled by Erdoğan as supporters of terrorism: "We know very well the ones that sheltered in their hotels those who cooperated with terror. If we do not hold them accountable, then the nation will hold us accountable."[3]

The dam truly burst in December 2013, when I was already back in the U.S. during my third season. In that month, Turkish police forces arrested top political figures in Erdoğan's party for being involved in bribery and money-laundering activities. Days later, Turkish media reported that the investigation was expanding to examine Erdoğan himself and his two sons. Fearful of what the investigation would uncover, in January 2014 Erdoğan removed hundreds of police officials from their posts, including those leading the investigation into the misdeeds. He said the probe was an international conspiracy orchestrated by my mentor, Mr. Fethullah Gülen (which, of course, was not true). Soon journalists reporting on the matter—many of whom were my friends—were thrown in jail, as were more police, judges, and prosecutors involved. Many schools in the Hizmet network—the beloved places where I had been intellectually formed—were being ordered to shut down. Erdoğan was punishing them because pro-Gülen media, with their massive audiences, were the only outlets with the courage to cover the story accurately.

I was infuriated. But I got even angrier one morning in February 2014 when I woke up at 5 a.m. to pray. I quickly checked Twitter before I began and saw that a secret recording had emerged of Erdoğan speaking with one of his sons, Bilal Erdoğan, commanding him to dispose of €30 million that was almost certainly embezzled from the Turkish people, validating the corruption investigation. That news, combined with the continued closures of Hizmet schools, was the last straw. *If you're fighting against the free press and shutting down schools, I have to say something,* I thought.

Ever since I first entered the NBA, I had maintained a Twitter account to post fun content for fans and follow the news. I never said anything political. But in this moment, disgusted at how Erdoğan's government of thugs was running the country, I embraced Twitter as an incredibly powerful outlet for me, as a famous Turkish citizen, to call out the regime's abuses. After I finished my morning prayers, I tweeted to my tens of thousands of followers something like, "I don't care who you are, but if you are fighting against education by shutting down schools and fighting against free media, then I'll hold you accountable and call you out." A few hours later, before the game that night, I was shocked to see that the tweet had gotten thousands of likes and retweets. I also saw how outraged Erdoğan's troll army on Twitter became, hurling vicious insults at me. Major U.S. media outlets started quoting me, and I saw that the more I talked, the more my views gained exposure. *American free speech is such a gift,* I remember thinking. *If I were back in Turkey, I'd be in jail by now.* After more than three years in America, I suddenly treasured the protections of constitutionally guaranteed freedoms, and saw them as my secret weapon in fighting Erdoğan.

I didn't know it at the time, but that moment was destined to become one of the most important of my life. It was the first time that I realized how much influence I could have in bringing the world's attention to the dictatorship festering inside my homeland. In the months to come, I started tweeting about injustices in Turkey more and more (mostly in Turkish), but the media wasn't really reporting on it.

Later that same month, February 2014, I had dinner in Utah with my friends Mehmet Okur and Hedo Türkoğlu, probably the biggest Turkish star in NBA history. Now on the tail end of his career, Hedo had always been friendly with me, especially because we had played together on the national team. But ever since I started criticizing Erdoğan on Twitter, he was getting colder.

Erdoğan had been on a rampage, shutting down media outlets and imprisoning officials and journalists poking their nose into a corruption scandal involving him, his family, and his political party. Turks in my home country and around the world were outraged at how our democracy was being torn apart. But somehow, Hedo had become a true Erdoğan supporter, ever since Erdoğan's people started getting friendly with him.

"Look, buddy," I told Hedo. "Erdoğan is using you."

"Why would he use me? He doesn't need me for anything. He's the prime minister."

"You've played in the NBA for fifteen years. You play for the national team. Everyone knows you. If he has you, he has your fans."

"I can't believe you're criticizing our prime minister like that! He's doing everything right."

Memo chimed in: "Even if I was dying, I wouldn't give him my vote."

"You're wrong," Hedo said with a shrug. "Erdoğan's going to be the best ever. I'm going to vote for him. And I'm going to encourage all of my fans to vote for him."

After dinner, I reflected on the conversation. If a man who had spent years in the free world like Hedo could be captured by Erdoğan's lies, then what would ordinary Turks be thinking about him?

That night, I decided that I had to get even more serious about my activism. But I had to get smarter on the issues.

Up to that time, I had spent most of my time off the court going to dinner and movies with teammates. Now after the games and practices were over, I would simply return to my hotel room each night to study the politics of Turkey and the Middle East. I realized that Erdoğan and his cronies had been stealing and improperly punishing political opponents for a long time. I became more motivated to speak out—not just because of my relationship with Gülen, but because I was a human being with a sense of right and wrong.

After the 2013–14 season ended, I went back to Turkey as usual. I hadn't really talked to my family about my new passion for speaking out against Erdoğan, so they wanted an explanation for why I was doing it. "There are so many innocent people in jail," I told them. "I can't stay quiet."

"Is this something you'll keep doing?" my mom asked nervously.

"I have to do something."

I originally intended to spend the whole summer in Turkey. But within two weeks of arriving, I realized how unsafe the streets were for me. The dirty looks I got in public matched the death threats I was starting to receive on social media whenever I condemned the Erdoğan regime: You son of a bitch. Those days will come when we will cut your head off and set it on fire on a spear, read one of them. I decided it was better to return to the U.S. for the rest of the summer, so I cut my trip short.

This period in my life also marked an evolution in my identity. It was astonishing to see the amount of support I received from fans in the U.S. for speaking up against the corruption in Turkey. Whereas many of my fellow Turks saw me as betraying the nation (or as an outright terrorist), Americans who knew what I was doing believed I was a hero for standing up to tyranny. Though I wasn't getting much media attention at this time, sometimes during the game or on a trip to the mall, fans would say things like, "Keep doing what you're doing. This is bigger than basketball." The encouragement fueled my outspokenness. Slowly but surely, I was beginning to regard America as my home, and the love of freedom was the fuel for this change. My teammates were not really for or against what I was doing. Frankly, it didn't really affect them. They just wanted to know what was going on. They were seeing the death threats on my Twitter account and got concerned for me and my family.

Training camp for the 2014–15 season began with a new teammate: Rudy Gobert, a 7'1" Frenchman who would go on to become a four-time defensive player of the year. Al Jefferson and Paul Millsap had decided to sign with other teams when their contracts expired, making me the starting center, and I would go on to average more than 15 points per game that year. But because Coach Quin Snyder wanted to give every big man a fair distribution of minutes, my minutes declined, and I hated not playing. And even though money has never been the most important part of my basketball career, I wasn't sure if the Jazz were going to offer me the large contract extension for which I would soon be eligible at the end of my fourth year.

Between my desire for more playing time and my growing desire to speak out on behalf of innocent people, I realized I needed to ask Utah for a trade. Many NBA players try to play in the biggest media markets so that they can enhance their personal brands. I slowly began to care more about going to a bigger city with more opportunities to generate attention on the issues I cared about. I still loved basketball, but with disturbing new reports of government-inflicted misery coming out of Turkey every day, politics was starting to move toward the center of my life. I understood the purpose of my life to be bigger than just putting a ball in a hoop, and I wanted to go to a place where I'd have a bigger platform to tell my story.

The next day the Jazz flew to Dallas for a game against the Mavericks, the final one before the annual All-Star break. I had previously made plans to fly to New York for the time off. In the meantime, I knew I wanted a trade but didn't know how to set one in motion. I also didn't want to tell my agent my real motivations for wanting out of Utah. After the game, I asked one of the reporters who covered the Jazz to hand me his iPhone for a moment. I opened the Notes app and typed in a single sentence: "Enes Kanter wants to get traded before the deadline."

The reporter was shocked: "Are you sure you want to do this?"

I told him to write up the story and release it in exactly one hour—at precisely the time I would be on a plane to New York.

He did as I asked, and all hell broke loose while I was in the air. When I landed, my agent, Max, called me.

"Are you crazy? What are you doing? You're going to kill your career!"

"I like to take risks," I calmly told him, and went on to detail my thinking.

Over the next few days in New York, I checked my phone multiple times per day in hopes of seeing a headline that I had been dealt before the trade deadline of February 19. For both basketball and political activism reasons, I didn't want to go back to Utah. But when it was time for the team to reassemble for our first game after the trade deadline, there I was.

As I awkwardly entered the practice facility for our first workout since the All-Star break, I saw a message on the team whiteboard in the locker room: "Welcome back, Enes. We love you." My buddy Derrick Favors had written it to let me know that my teammates were still my family despite the trade request. Once we got on the floor for practice, Coach Snyder stared right at me, and my heart dropped into my stomach. He pulled me aside. "You still might get traded tomorrow. We don't need you to join practice and hurt yourself. Just run on the sidelines."

Even though holding me back from practice was a smart move to preserve my trade value, I was sad to be separated from the pack. All the other players were laughing at me. One assistant coach, thinking I had acted selfishly by saying I wanted out of Utah, told me that I should be ashamed of myself. That night, I went home and watched the minutes until the deadline tick by.

Practice was scheduled for 1:30 p.m. the next day—thirty minutes after the trade deadline. All morning I stayed at my house and refreshed the ESPN site regularly, thirsting for some news. At 12:50 p.m., seeing nothing, I gave up hope and got into my car to head to practice. Then, at 12:59—one minute before the deadline—the star NBA reporter Adrian Wojnarowski tweeted that I would be headed to the Oklahoma City Thunder. Although it wasn't a city with a massive media market like I hoped for, I was elated at this news, because the Thunder were an up-and-coming team headlined by the incredible young duo of Kevin Durant and Russell Westbrook. That alone generated more attention on the team than it would have normally had. The next day, the Thunder sent a private jet to pick me up.

An exciting new chapter in my basketball career was beginning. But elsewhere in my life, misery was about to begin.

CHAPTER 7

ERDOĞAN'S REVENGE

What are we doing here? I wondered.

It was a freezing February day during my first week with my new team, the Oklahoma City Thunder. I had expected to go straight to the team's practice facility, but I instead found myself standing outside in the cold with Sam Presti, the Thunder's general manager. My new teammates Steve Novak, D. J. Augustin, Kyle Singler, and I were staring at a large reflecting pool in the middle of downtown Oklahoma City, with little idea of why I was here.

Then Presti told us what this was all about: "This is the memorial to the victims of the Oklahoma City Bombing. This is the first place we take every new player. We want you to know what this city has been through. We want you to understand that you are fighting for these people."

On April 19, 1995, Timothy McVeigh and Terry Nichols committed a despicable act of terrorism against their own country, detonating a truck bomb underneath the Alfred P. Murrah Federal Building in Oklahoma City. One hundred sixty-eight people were killed, including children, and at least 680 were wounded, making it the worst terrorist attack in U.S.

history before 9/11. The community was shattered by the bloodshed, and the attack left deep scars across the city. Even though America is completely exceptional as a place where politics overwhelmingly happens peacefully, there are still nutcases who think that acts of violence are the best way to preserve American ideals. In fact, nothing is less American.

For this part of the afternoon, Presti was basically a tour guide, explaining all of this to me. I was deeply moved by the experience of visiting the memorial, and I never forgot that day throughout my entire time with the Thunder. Each time I stepped on the court, I reminded myself of what the fans here had suffered, and gave my all for them.

My time in Oklahoma began on that sad note, but I was thrilled to be with my new team after being traded from the Jazz. During my first day in practice, future Hall of Famers Russell Westbrook and Kevin Durant gave me hugs and welcomed me to the Thunder family. I had never played with true superstars before, and meeting Russ and KD made me realize that I now had teammates who were on another level. Besides their talent, Russ and Kevin were incredible teammates. When I met Durant for the first time, he shook my hand and said, "Let's get it done, big man." I instantly flashed back to the day years before when I met him at the Nike camp in New York. I was living the dream. I also loved my new coach, Scott Brooks, a great basketball mind and highly approachable guy.

The best part of being with the Thunder was the playing time I was getting. Unfortunately, it was largely due to injuries. Center Steven Adams, who would become my best friend in the NBA, broke his hand not long before I arrived, so I immediately had a big role. A week later, Durant suffered a foot injury that kept him out for the rest of the season. Serge Ibaka, a young power forward, also went down. Soon Russell Westbrook and I were carrying the team, and he and I developed outstanding chemistry. Over the rest of that season, I played well enough to be rewarded with a maximum-dollar contract extension that summer. Playing beside Westbrook in his prime definitely helped make that happen! Off the court, Russ and I got to be friends—we lived about two minutes from each other, so we played a lot of video games together in our downtime. We also loved to eat my favorite food, *maklube*, a Turkish meat and rice dish that is sometimes, and for stupid reasons, associated with terrorists in Turkey. The next day, the pro-Erdoğan news outlets proclaimed that Russ wasn't welcome in Turkey. What a juvenile response!

The Thunder's organizational culture was by far the best I experienced in the NBA. Setting the tone was Presti, a man so committed to perfection that he got his hair cut twice a week. Sam had previously been part of the San Antonio Spurs organization, which is also famous for having a culture of excellence. After arriving in Oklahoma City, he made sure no one in the organization overlooked a single detail in his or her work. The lawn at the practice facility was perfectly manicured. Ball boys were ordered to make sure every basketball sitting on a rack had the logo facing the same direction. And the players got whatever they felt they needed to be at their best: one guy asked for a certain kind of water from New Zealand, and the team spent $100,000 to import it for him.

In my case, the team eagerly accommodated my Muslim beliefs. The team provided me with a prayer room in both the practice facility and the arena so that I could pray whenever I needed to. The Thunder also began bringing halal food into the locker room for my postgame meal, both at home and on the road. Soon the other guys discovered how delicious the kebabs, *köfte*, and other Middle Eastern foods were. Before long the team was ordering huge amounts of halal food for us. The *Wall Street Journal* even did a story on our team's love of halal Turkish food, and Kevin Durant joked, "I've been here for nine years and I requested some stuff after the game and I have to pay for it on my own. And the second [Enes] gets here he gets his own menu."[1]

Perhaps most touching was the way the team worked with me as I fasted during the Muslim holiday of Ramadan. Not eating or drinking during daylight makes it very difficult for a pro athlete to get the hydration and calories he needs during the day. I would wake up every morning around 3 or 4 a.m. and pound water and food before the day began. At night, after the sun went down, I would force myself to eat as much as possible, even scarfing down food on the team bus before ordering room service as soon as I got back to the hotel. One night, before a game that began after sundown, I ate six peanut butter and jelly sandwiches for some last-minute energy. It wasn't fun, but one of the Thunder's lifting coaches kindly fasted for three days alongside me so that he could understand how I felt. He then put together a strength training plan that would work for me during Ramadan.[2]

The Thunder was a true brotherhood, on and off the court, and I was so happy in my new city. Durant, Russ, and most of the other members of the team had been to Turkey before, and we had many talks about my home country. The Thunder, like many NBA teams, also held chapel, and I often attended with my teammates so that I could learn about Christianity and hear the pastor's sermon. Everyone would pray and hug together afterward, a special moment indeed, and one that was impossible to imagine on a religiously diverse team anywhere else in the world. Oklahoma City is cowboy country (or what remains of it) and the heartland of evangelical Christianity in America. But everyone in the Thunder organization was eager to make sure I felt comfortable—yet more evidence that America is a land where not everyone believes the same thing, but most people are eager to treat people of different religions with respect.

My first season with the Thunder wrapped up in June 2015 as a disappointment for the team. Because of all the injuries, we barely missed the playoffs. Unfortunately, as often happens in the NBA, someone had to be made a scapegoat for a team that was supposed to contend for a title. Coach Brooks was soon fired. I was disappointed that such a gifted teacher of the game and leader was tossed aside. Fortunately, Scott landed another head-coaching gig with the Washington Wizards and made several playoff appearances with them.

Late June 2015 brought the first retaliatory actions by the Erdoğan mafia against me. Although I had played for the national team for years, when the roster for the Turkish national team that was being assembled ahead of the 2015 summer's European Championship was released, I discovered that I wasn't on it. I can't say I was surprised, but it still hurt. The coach, Ergin Ataman, said I was omitted because I hadn't apologized to teammates for "past incidents," which was not true at all.[3] Sure, the national team was still mad at me because I decided not to play in 2013 to let the broken bone in my shoulder get better. But the real reason I wasn't on the team was my outspoken political views and opposition to Erdoğan's maniac ways. Erdoğan had given an order to the national team executives to deny me a roster spot because of my association with Fethullah Gülen. I didn't take the news quietly. The reason I was not included in the squad is the values I believe in and my political stance, I wrote on Twitter.

Being left off the national team was just the first indication of the whole country turning its back on me. That summer, once again visiting Turkey, I felt the eyes of the Turkish street staring daggers at me. The Turkish athletic world was jealous that someone who they thought was a traitor was now the highest-paid Turkish athlete of all time after I signed a maximum-salary contract extension with the Thunder in July. Nonetheless, I continued criticizing the Erdoğan regime, and soon people in the Turkish political world who agreed with me started sending me direct messages. Through these DMs I started to grow my personal contacts with police and people in the judicial world, including Zekeriya Öz, one of the tireless prosecutors putting pressure on Erdoğan and his gang. He and others gave me encouragement to use my role as a high-profile athlete to keep speaking out publicly.

It wasn't long before innocent people paid the price for our connections. In August 2015, I posted a picture of me with Zekeriya Öz and Celal Kara, the prosecutor who initiated the corruption and bribery investigation of 2013 (and was later fired for it). That made the Erdoğan trolls on Twitter have a meltdown. Security soon became a greater and greater concern. A day or so after I posted the picture of us, Öz fired his bodyguard because he suspected him of leaking things to the pro-Erdoğan camp. In 2016, the police detained my dentist, who had let me, Zekeriya, and Celal use his balcony to take our picture. He and his wife were kept in jail for a year and a half before he was given a seven-and-a-half-year sentence on charges of being members of a "terrorist group." They remain there today. Öz had to seek asylum in Germany later that year.

In the Kanter household, the consequences of my actions were hurting my brother Ahmet Said, who had hoped to follow his big brother into the NBA. He was blossoming as a talented player, but mysteriously had trouble sticking on various teams he played on.

"Enes, I'm the best one on my team. I'm the tallest one. Why am I getting kicked off every team?" he wondered. I didn't have the heart to tell him that coaches and teammates were bullying him and kicking him off every team because of his last name.

Thankfully, Ahmet has since been able to come to America and play some semipro ball, but I don't think his career is what it should have been for his level of talent. The Turkish government's pressure robbed him of a chance to properly develop as a basketball player. My other brother, Kerem, had already come to the U.S. in 2013 and wound up playing four years of Division I ball for the University of Wisconsin–Green Bay and Xavier. I'm incredibly proud that he's continued his basketball career in France, Spain, Greece, Poland, and Japan.

As the summer wound down and I prepared to return to the U.S. for the 2015–16 season, I had a meeting with my mom and dad. I had made up my mind that there was no turning back for me in my righteous anger against the Erdoğan regime. "I am going to take a path that will not be easy for any of us," I began. "You might get threats, death threats, jail, or abuse in the news. You won't walk comfortably outside the house. If you aren't okay with this, let me know."

My mom, who has a moral core made of iron, simply stated, "If you are standing for the truth, we are with you until the end."

My dad, perhaps seeing how his life was about to be destroyed, didn't say anything. He simply put his head down in his hands. Because of an onslaught of online death threats I was receiving at that time ("I hired a serial killer to kill you. Soon I will prove it to you"), I bought a plane ticket to leave the very next day. "You're not coming back after this," my mom prophesied.

A day later, when a taxi pulled up to take me to the airport, I climbed in and gazed through the back window at my mother and sister standing on the balcony of my family's apartment, both of them waving goodbye to me. Somehow I knew that this would be the last time I'd see my family for a long time.

I mumbled to myself, "I hope this isn't the last time I'm seeing you, Mom. But if it is, take care. I'll always love you."

To this day, I'm still waiting for a reunion.

With Scott Brooks fired at the end of the 2014–15 season, Billy Donovan took over as the Thunder's head coach for the 2015–16 campaign. Although Billy had never coached at the NBA level, he had won back-to-back NCAA championships with the Florida Gators in 2006 and 2007. Sam thought he was the guy best suited to lead the Thunder to their first-ever title. It was true that Billy was a great X's and O's coach, but he wasn't NBA-ready. Among other flaws, he held the stars to a different standard than the rest of us. Whenever Russ or KD made a mistake in practice, he would let it go. Moments later, whenever another player screwed up, he would start screaming at them to make the point he should have made to the superstars. The players did not take this well—Serge Ibaka and Billy got in many screaming matches over the course of the second year. Billy was also kind of an awkward guy whom the players felt tense talking to.

By the time the playoffs came around, the locker room had lost a lot of respect for him.

Before the 2015–16 season began, our team played an exhibition game in Oklahoma City against Fenerbahçe, the team that had helped sabotage my chances of playing college basketball. Before the game started, the İstiklal Marşı, the Turkish national anthem, played. For two minutes I beamed with pride for my home country, but also felt a stab of sadness from missing it. Erdoğan's persecution of me also influenced my interactions with the Fenerbahçe players, many of whom were my friends. They didn't say a word to me during the game, because they were too afraid of the backlash they would receive in Turkey if they were photographed shaking hands with me. Because Fenerbahçe is a well-known team, many Turkish Americans who cheer for them attended. They were treated to the Thunder blowing away one of the best teams in Europe by 30 points. None of the Fenerbahçe players greeted any of their own fans after the game because they were afraid that I would be saying hello to them too.

The 2015–16 Thunder were a great team, finishing third in the Western Conference with 55 wins. In the first round, we blew past Dirk Nowitzki and the Dallas Mavericks 4 games to 1. Dirk couldn't guard anyone but was almost unstoppable as an offensive player. Besides Kareem Abdul-Jabbar's hook shot, Dirk's fadeaway, one-footed jumper, released from the hands of a man who stood seven feet tall, is probably the most difficult shot to block in NBA history. It was an honor to guard Dirk from time to time over the years, even when he sometimes tortured me.

The second round presented a harder test in the San Antonio Spurs, who had won the title two seasons before and were still a formidable opponent. They really worried us, and Presti had constructed our team in part to compete with their twin towers of Tim Duncan and LaMarcus Aldridge. It was so fun going to war with them alongside Steven Adams. Although San Antonio beat us by 32 in the first game, we took the series in six games. Immediately after the final game, the media started chattering that this was Duncan's last-ever game, a prediction that soon came true.

I turned to Steven and said, "We made a legend retire!" Steven rolled his eyes. "I don't think it was because *we* guarded him."

The only thing standing in our way en route to the NBA Finals was the Golden State Warriors. The Warriors, led by Steph Curry, Klay Thompson, Draymond Green, and Andre Iguodala, had won an NBA-record 73 regular season games that year. But we still thought we were the better team, and we almost proved it. We went up 3–1 in the series and began daydreaming of our Finals appearance.

Before Game 5, assistant coach Maurice Cheeks firmly told us in the locker room: "Do not relax. If they win one game, they will wake up. Do not let them get this." But our team was still young, and I don't think we took his warning seriously enough. By that time, everyone was already talking about the next round, and our focus was already lost. We blew Game 5. Still, everyone was confident that we would win Game 6 in front of our rabid home crowd. But I knew where this could lead. "Don't relax," I told my guys. "This is not guaranteed."

In Game 6, Golden State sharpshooter Klay Thompson caught fire, scoring 41 points from all over the court. No one could have stopped him, but we made some dumb turnovers in the final few minutes, and before we knew it we had lost. Afterward, no one could believe that we had blown this one. We had a team huddle in the locker room to try to forget about it and reset for Game 7, but now the pressure was becoming too much to bear, and Golden State had stolen back the momentum.

Before Game 7 in San Francisco, everyone on the Thunder was still shocked and in a bad mood. It was not the mindset necessary to win a do-or-die game. The game itself was a defensive battle. But Steph Curry (7 three-pointers) and Klay Thompson (6) still tortured us from deep on their way to a 96–88 victory. Everyone was crying in the locker room afterward, even me. Coach Donovan, through tears himself, told us how proud he was of us and how much heart we had shown throughout the season, but no one was really listening. But even after our failure, when our plane touched down back in Oklahoma City, thousands of fans had gathered at the airport to welcome us home and thank us for an excellent season. They are perhaps the most loyal in all of the NBA. They also respect the game—their standing ovation for Kobe Bryant in his final season was one of the most earsplitting moments I'd ever heard in any NBA arena.

Although my teammates and I were crushed by how the 2015–16 season ended, our near trip to the finals made all of us hungry to run it back the next year. Steven Adams and I began working hard shortly after the season ended to get in the best possible physical and mental shape for next year's grind. My teammates and I all assumed that our squad would stay intact and challenge for a title.

Then free agency started.

Every year, players whose contracts expire have a chance to sign with other teams. We knew that Kevin Durant's deal was up, but we all assumed he'd be back in a Thunder jersey.

So, imagine the shock waves that went through me when I saw a story that Durant had decided to leave Oklahoma City for our enemy, the Golden State Warriors. The Warriors were already the Avengers. They didn't need another superhero.

I was in an airport when I saw the news on Twitter. I thought it was a fake account spreading rumors. Then I saw the blue checkmark. I clicked through to the story and kept refreshing the page. It was true.

I texted Steven Adams.

> Dude, have you seen the news?
>
> Yeah. I can't believe it.

We were feeling distraught and betrayed, as if a brother had abandoned us. Most players on the team lost respect for Durant. He decided to join the team that was already the best in the NBA, while the Thunder were climbing up the mountain to knock them off the throne. We concluded that the media had gotten in his head with talk about his legacy, and he felt unnecessary pressure to chase a title before it was too late. The media had also fired him up by putting out fake speculation about animosity between him and Westbrook. While the two didn't hate each other, it was hard for two alpha dogs to exist on the same team.

The disappointment of KD leaving reverberated throughout the organization. But this was to be far from the worst thing that happened to me in the summer of 2016.

"Excuse me, but you need to see this."

On July 15, 2016, I was making a regular visit to Fethullah Gülen, the Turkish Islamic scholar living in exile in Pennsylvania. I was enjoying the beautiful summer day in conversation with him, a man whose teachings continue to inspire me. Then one of his young students burst into the room with an iPad.

"Something big is happening in Turkey!"

We huddled around the device, glued to the coverage from a Turkish news station. We couldn't believe it: members of the Turkish Armed Forces had, we were told, staged a coup against the Erdoğan-led Turkish government. Gülen then calmly addressed his young pupil:

"Tell all our friends around the world to stop whatever they're doing and to pray for the safety of Turkey and pray that innocent people don't get hurt."

Then Gülen, who consistently practices what he preaches, gathered us in our own prayer for our nation and a reading of the Islamic holy book of the Quran. The Quran reading was in Arabic, but I heard him pray in Turkish for the safety of our country and the Turkish people.

Two hours later, Erdoğan took to the airwaves calling the coup a conspiracy against him orchestrated by Gülen. Everyone's face sank in shock and horror—not to mention disbelief. I was sitting next to Gülen when the news broke, and I can tell you that he was sitting and praying, not pulling the strings of power back home. And just to show you that Gülen wasn't living lavishly off his followers, his private room at the compound where his students also studied was furnished only with a mattress, a space heater, and piles of books.[4]

Erdoğan's fake news also caused American and foreign media outlets to rush to the retreat center Gülen lived in. Helicopters and drones buzzed overhead. Hundreds of people gathered at the front gate of the center, including pro-Erdoğan thugs. Gülen pleaded with all his guests to not leave the residence, fearing that we might be attacked upon leaving, or that a mob would rush inside as soon as they opened up the gates.

The day after the attempted coup, and with Erdoğan's disinformation spreading like a virus, Gülen decided to give a press conference to an array of international media outlets to refute the lies. He urged that an independent international commission be assembled to determine who masterminded the coup and promised that he would gladly return to Turkey if credible evidence pointed to him or his followers. "If there is a forceful desire for me to leave, then you know here I will leave no problem," he explained. "But I don't think that the Turkish government will be able to produce credible evidence."[5]

Gülen's refusal to give in to the false narrative gave incredible motivation to his followers to resist it as well. We would need it, because the Erdoğan regime soon started a program of mass persecution that made a mockery of Turkey's democracy and his claim to be a democratic leader. In the months and years to come, the regime arrested tens of thousands of Turkish citizens suspected of being affiliated with the Hizmet movement, and suspended or fired thousands more from their jobs. Scores of journalists were put in jail, and the atmosphere of the country moved closer to being a police state. My life—already the object of Erdoğan's obsession—was about to become even more difficult.

My dad was one of the early victims of the purge against all suspected Hizmet-affiliated people working in the government. A few weeks after the coup, he was removed from his position as a university professor. One of the worst parts about it—besides the fact that my dad is one of the most brilliant scientists in Turkey—is that he was two months away from being eligible to retire with a pension. Erdoğan's regime moved fast to terminate him before he could collect a cent. Other members of my extended family also lost their jobs.

In return, my family put out their own statement disowning me.[6] "I apologize to the Turkish people and the president for having such a son," my dad wrote. "His statements and behavior trouble our family. I would not have taken Enes to the U.S. for the basketball camp where his talent was discovered had I known that it would come to this point." I went to a practice with some of my teammates later that day. I knew from the looks on their faces that they wanted to ask me about the situation but realized that it was so personal and painful for me, they kept quiet.

In response, on August 8, I temporarily changed my name on Twitter to Enes Gülen and wrote,

> Today I lost my mother, father, brothers and sisters, my family and all my relatives. My own father asked me to change my surname. My mother, who has given me life, disowned me. My brothers and sisters with which we have grown together ignore me. My relatives don't want to see me again.[7]

The Turkish government was happy to see my family's letter and used it as propaganda to show the Turkish people that even my own family didn't want me. But the government suspected that my family had issued the statement only to be left alone. Not long after, the police raided my family's house. They trashed the entire place looking for evidence that I had coordinated with my family members to put out a bogus statement. By the time the cops were done, they had seized every phone, tablet, and computer in the house, even the one my sister tried to flush down the toilet in the seconds when the police burst in. The only thing the police would find if they searched that phone were messages between her and me about how our summers were going.

The Erdoğan regime's unjust abuses after the coup were so egregious that I felt I personally needed to bring them to the attention of members of the U.S. Congress. Because Turkey is a U.S. ally in NATO and a key player in the Middle East, many members of Congress have a serious interest in the country's trajectory. They needed to know the truth about Gülen and the coup.

A lobbyist friend of mine reached out to his contacts in Washington—the White House, Congress, FBI, State Department, etc.—and convened an unofficial meeting on Capitol Hill for me to share what I knew about the coup. Most members of Congress knew that the Turkish government had not sent one shred of credible evidence to the U.S. or any other Western government that indicated Gülen was behind it. "This is what dictators do," one of them stated. "They pick a target and make it a scapegoat."

Another one said, "When Gülen came here for the first time, he and his people were knocking on church and synagogue doors to meet their neighbors and sharing food with poor people. You don't have to worry." It relieved me to hear him reassure his colleagues that Gülen was not a puppet master who had pulled off a coup. It was also inspiring to see that American politicians didn't just care about the health of democracy in their own country—they also took pains to support the Turkish people's freedoms. For all the nasty things said about Congress these days, there are still good people on both sides of the aisle.

For the 2016–17 season, now missing one of the most elite scorers in NBA history, the Thunder slipped in the standings the next year, finishing sixth in the Western Conference and losing in the first round of the playoffs to the Houston Rockets. The Rockets now were led by prime James Harden. In addition to being the first-ever NBA player to dunk on me, Harden was the most unguardable player in the league at this time. He averaged 33 points per game in the series and sent us home.

But something incredible happened during this year. Russell Westbrook averaged a triple double—double-digit points, rebounds, and assists—for an entire season. He also broke Oscar Robertson's record for triple doubles in a season, notching 42 of them. This was just one of many records he smashed that year. During some games, my teammates and I would stare at each other in disbelief as Russ piled up stats—*Did he really do that again?* I was very happy to be part of his journey, which ended with him winning the MVP Award. On the day he received the award, I stood with Steven Adams on the court behind Russ as Commissioner Adam Silver handed him the trophy. We were so proud of Russ—and our part in helping him attain such an honor. He deserved the world for what he achieved that season.

As great as that year was, the lowlight of the season for me personally came at the end of January, when I punched a chair in frustration as I came off the court after a bad possession. Players punch chairs all the time, so that's nothing new. But I missed the soft padding on the back of the folding chair and instead slammed my fist into the metal frame. The price I paid was a broken forearm that kept me out for ten games. Steven Adams smacked my head when I told him the X-ray showed a break. I thought Sam Presti would be furious and fine me. Instead he only admonished me, saying, "You need to learn from this." He was right. This kind of outburst couldn't happen again so that I didn't hurt myself and, more importantly, the team.

That offseason, I continued to take my basketball camps international—something I had first done the year before. That year, I visited fifteen countries in about forty days. It was a beautiful thing bringing smiles to kids' faces through the language of basketball. I resolved to make 2017's tour even bigger and better, including a leg in the Asia-Pacific region. People warned me that in certain countries, people can hire a hit man to take someone out for as little as $125. That number kept rattling in my head as I wondered if cold-blooded Turkish intelligence operatives would hire someone desperate enough to kill another human being for such a small sum.

As I described in the beginning of this book, Turkey did come after me, just not in the way I expected. They tried to get the Indonesian security services to grab me a day before my twenty-fifth birthday, on May 19, 2017. Over the next few days (which were truly one big sleep-deprived blur), I fled from Jakarta to Singapore to Bucharest to London to New York. In the middle of the nightmare, in Romania, I posted a video to Twitter to tell the world what was happening: They've been holding us here for hours by these two police. The reason behind it of course is my political views. The guy who did it is Recep Tayyip Erdoğan, the president of Turkey. . . . I'll keep you posted guys, but just pray for us, and I'll tell you what's going on.[8]

The video blew up, and friends and family instantly texted me. Let me know what I can do, Russell Westbrook wrote. He also helped get the #FreeEnes hashtag trending on Twitter. When Mel and I finally made it back to the U.S., I was never so happy to see the "Welcome to the United States of America" sign. I had missed being forcibly returned to Turkey by the skin of my teeth, maybe never to be heard from again. I tweeted a picture of me posing in front of the sign, along with a message:

> Well!!
> Hello
> The most beautiful country in the world.
> The United States of America.

The day after I returned to the United States, I held a press conference at the National Basketball Players Association headquarters. "Erdoğan, he's a terrible man. He's the Hitler of our century," I said.[9] "I hope the world is going to do something about it." The outpouring of support from so many fans and teammates both during and after the ordeal was incredible, and it triggered a shift in my national allegiance. "I'm not even from America, and I see all these people and I get all this support. I feel like this is my home now," I remarked. "I am going to try to become an American citizen."[10]

But for the time being, with my Turkish passport confiscated, I was a man without a country. A day after the press conference, I went on *CBS This Morning* to share my experience. The hosts remarked that Erdoğan had arrested 120 journalists, closed more than 150 news outlets, and jailed more than 140,000 people since the coup. "I stand for what I believe. I want to be the voice of all these innocent people."[11]

You'd think that this episode would have caused Erdoğan to let up for a bit. No chance. Less than a week later, the Istanbul prosecutor's office asked a court to sign off on an arrest warrant for me, on the grounds of "being a member of a terrorist organization." I was learning that this would be my life from now on.[12]

Even worse, in June 2017, the government threw my dad into jail on fake charges of supporting terrorism. The moment I heard the news from my brother Kerem, I flashed back to the conversation I had with my parents on my final (to date) trip to Turkey: "This is the road I'm going down. Your lives will not be the same."

Kerem asked me, "How do you think they'll treat him?"

I told him, "I don't know, but there's nothing we can do for him inside."

Fortunately, my dad was released not long after. But this wasn't a happy ending—it was just an initial detention as he awaited a trial. When I talked to my brother after my dad came home, he sounded extremely anxious about what might have happened. "Dad doesn't act the same," he sighed. "He won't talk about it. He spends the day staring at the walls and acting weird. Maybe he was tortured. Maybe they gave him some kind of drugs. But he's not the same."

For months afterward, my dad was hauled before a sadistic judge who threatened him with bizarre punishments like making him wear a skirt and dance in public. I wished I could be with my dad to comfort him. But I couldn't travel to Turkey. And I haven't been able to talk with him since 2016.

CHAPTER 8

STANDING ON PRINCIPLE

By the end of the 2016–17 season, I was a full-fledged NBA veteran. Even though I was only twenty-four years old, I'd been in the league six years already. I'd known what it was to win, to lose, to be traded, to be injured, to endure 3 a.m. cross-country flights every week, and so much more.

In short, NBA life was a business. And on September 25, 2017, I was reminded of that fact once again.

A few weeks before training camp for the 2017–18 season, I was running a basketball camp for special needs kids in the Oklahoma City area. After 2015, when I realized it would be impossible to continue visiting Turkey again, I started using my time off to inspire kids in America and all over the world. Basketball was my platform to bring people of various races and religions together and spread positive energy. The game teaches kids how to develop winning strategies, how to communicate, and how to work as a team. After the games, I loved taking questions from the kids about stuff happening off the court—things like life, the world, growing up. That's what mattered the most.

On this particular day, I was having a blast interacting with the kids and streaming the fun on Instagram Live. I started seeing loads of comments on my feed saying things like, "Let's go Knicks!" I couldn't figure out why so many Knicks fans were commenting, but whatever.

Then my manager, Hank, approached me at midcourt during a break in the action.

"You just got traded to the Knicks for Carmelo Anthony," he whispered in my ear.

This was mostly good news. I felt heartbreak that I was leaving the best organization I could ever have been a part of, but I understood that the Thunder needed to add some scoring punch to replace Durant. Carmelo could fill it up with the best of them, and the Thunder were planning on giving Steven Adams more minutes at center anyway. Frankly, it was flattering to know that the Knicks thought that I was a good prize in exchange for one of the top scorers in league history. Soon Sam Presti, a guy who genuinely cares about his players, called me. "We love you, Enes. Thank you for all you've done for the team and the community. New York will be the big market you've always wanted." I gave Sam my love back, and that was that.

People thought that I'd want to cancel the two additional camps I was planning to hold that day as I processed the news. But I had hundreds of kids coming, and I didn't want to let them down. Showing that the bond we had developed was bigger than basketball, Steven Adams and Russell Westbrook showed up to the second camp and the kids went wild. I'll never forget their generosity that day.

Afterward, we three went out to eat and laughed over stories of our time together. One hilarious tale was about Serge Ibaka, who came to the NBA at age twenty after growing up in the Congo. Ibaka's English at that time was not smooth, and he knew practically nothing of how things work in the U.S. After signing his first contract with the Thunder, he looked at his pay stub and saw tens of thousands of dollars deducted from his check. Serge broke into a rage and demanded to know from the team's accountants, "What happened to all my money?!"

"Uncle Sam took his share," they told him.

Still furious, Serge went and pounded on the door of Sam Presti's office: "You tricked me! You need to give me my money!"

Sam was completely confused. "I don't have any of your money! What are you talking about?"

"They told me that Uncle Sam had taken some of my money—that's you!"

Sam laughed and began to explain to Serge that Uncle Sam is a nickname for the U.S. government, which takes its share of players' earnings for tax purposes.

Being shipped to the Big Apple presented the chance to finally play under the bright lights of Madison Square Garden, something I'd longed to do ever since I first visited New York when I was sixteen. I had to pinch myself that celebrities like Jimmy Fallon, Trevor Noah, Shakira, Ronaldo, Ben Stiller, and Tracy Morgan came to the Garden to watch us play. Suiting up beside me were up-and-comers like Tim Hardaway Jr. and the ultragifted Kristaps Porziņģis. Of course, New York was most appealing because of its massive status as a hub of global media. I knew that I could put a much brighter spotlight on all the turmoil happening in my home country. I wanted every American to know that I was fighting against a dictator, and for human rights everywhere. As I got to know my new teammates, I slowly explained what had happened to me in Indonesia and why. They couldn't believe it: "Man, are you serious? That's crazy!"

During the summer, besides getting fat from eating too much of my favorite Turkish food ("I needed like a bra or something," I said to one newspaper),[1] I had continued my activism on behalf of innocent Turks held in Erdoğan's dungeons.

I also turned to issues in America. On August 12, during a rally of Nazis, Ku Klux Klan members, and other racists in Charlottesville, Virginia, a sick individual rammed his car into a bunch of counterprotesters, killing one woman and injuring thirty-five others. It opened my eyes to see that America had more work to do. I called upon other athletes, saying,

"What's happening in America is more important than your contract, is more important than your endorsement deal, whatever."[2]

In October 2017, when NFL players were taking a knee during the national anthem, my teammates and I met to discuss what we should do. We decided to link arms together during the anthem for the first preseason game. I told the press, "In America it doesn't matter—anywhere in the world it doesn't matter—tall, short, black, white, fat, skinny, whatever you are, we need to work this out together."[3] I still believe that we must unite in spite of our differences.

Meanwhile, I kept fighting for innocent Turks, to predictable results. Seven months after my incident in Indonesia, Turkey came after me again. At the end of December 2017, the government, acting on the indictment prepared by the Istanbul prosecutor in June, issued an arrest warrant for me, calling me a terrorist for my relationship with Gülen and his followers. They wanted to throw me in jail for four years. I sneered at the threat. "Only four years? All the trash I've been talking?" I scoffed to the *New York Post*. "I'm just trying to be the voice of all of these innocent people, man."[4]

Being in America gave me a safe haven from Erdoğan's reach, but the rest of my family wasn't so fortunate. They continued to suffer political persecution. When my mom went out of the house, people spat in her face and told her, "Your son is a terrorist!" My dad was also spit on, and kicked out of a mosque in Istanbul. People in the town of Erciş, near my hometown of Van, demanded that the local Bedir Mosque, which our family had helped fund, and which Gülen had named, be demolished. The townspeople were so insistent on its destruction that they even offered the head imam money to carry out the plot. Thankfully, he had the good sense to tell them, "You can change the name of the mosque if you want, but there's no way I'm knocking it down. This is the house of God."

In 2018, things got even worse as I plowed full steam ahead. In June my stomach turned as I learned that my father was sentenced to fifteen years in prison for a crime he never committed. I told the world, "No matter what happens, I will continue to keep fighting for human rights and freedom of speech, justice and democracy above all. I will stand for what I believe in. All I'm doing is trying to be the voice of all those innocent people."[5]

By the grace of God (and the pressure of the international media), my dad was freed in 2020. But the Kanter family still suffers to this day. My sister, Betül, a brilliant woman who completed six years of medical school, cannot not get hired anywhere. My dad probably has post-traumatic stress disorder (PTSD) and is banned from working. The Turkish government has confiscated each family member's passport, preventing them from leaving the country. Each day the security services watch them closely. If they contact me directly, the government will have grounds to put them in jail for having contact with a terrorist. They could risk leaving Turkey illegally, but the punishment for getting caught crossing the border without proper authorization could be life imprisonment—or a bullet in the back.

Being in a bigger market meant more chances to draw attention to the plight of my fellow citizens in Turkey. But it didn't mean more wins. We won only 29 games my first year, largely because Kristaps missed 34 games with injuries and Coach Jeff Hornacek was fired. When my second year in New York began, I was excited to make the most of my opportunity to play lots of minutes and prove to the fans that I was a worthy replacement for the legendary Carmelo Anthony.

Then I heard some rumors I'd never heard in my career.

The 2018–19 Knicks weren't expected to do well. In training camp, the players began talking among themselves in the locker room. "Forget about the playoffs," one said. "Our team just isn't good. I bet the management will try to tank."

"What's a tank?" I asked.

"It's when you lose on purpose."

"That won't happen in the NBA!" I exclaimed. "We're getting paid to try and win."

"Watch and see what happens," he warned.

I got off to a hot start that year, playing the best ball of my professional career. I put up double doubles regularly in the first 25 games, including nights of 23 (points) and 21 (rebounds), 21 and 19, and 21 and 26. But around the time when the team stood at a pathetic 9–27, in late December, Coach David Fizdale called me into his office and told me to sit down.

"Look, this is what happens when you're a good player on a bad team. From now on we're gonna sit you. We want to give our young guys an opportunity. So we're not gonna play you."

"What?!"

"You can yell and curse at me if you want to, but that's the deal. You aren't even going to start anymore."

I left his office shaking with rage. I couldn't believe that the team would lose on purpose! At practice that day I worked out poorly, being so down and frustrated at the situation. The other disappointing factor in all this was that I was entering another contract year, so I knew how a lack of playing time would affect my ability to get a new deal.

Being quiet about riding the bench when I was playing so well was never an option for me. One day after the New Year there was a media scrum in the locker room. I was sick of bottling up my frustration at not playing, all so that the Knicks could try to secure a higher draft pick. So I told the press I wanted to talk.

The Knicks media staffer tried to kill the idea, saying, "Enes hasn't been playing, so maybe he shouldn't talk."

This was like telling sharks not to chase a fish leaking a trail of blood. The New York media is the most savage in the country, and Russell Westbrook had even told me before I came to the city to watch out for them. Fortunately, they weren't out to burn me on this occasion. They wanted to hear from me why I wasn't starting all of a sudden, while the team sat at 9–29, the worst record in the league.

As I summoned the reporters over to my locker, the media guy muttered under his breath to me, "Don't do it. This is your contract year." He knew I was planning to unload. So did my teammates, who stopped what they were doing to listen to me.

Before any reporter could even blurt out a question, I told them, "I want this team to get to the playoffs one day. This is in my blood, man, I'm sorry. If anyone asks anything else, I'm not going to do it. I'm going out there to get a win every time. This organization is paying me. I don't want no free money. So every time I'm out there I'm going to try to get a win."[6] As I spoke, I saw the Knicks media guy with his hands buried in his face. He knew the blowback to this would not be good.

The unspoken part behind all this was that the Knicks were tanking, and I would not stand for it. That night, every sports media outlet in New York was talking about tanking, and the fans, who had caught on to the intentional losing by now, were in an uproar.

The next day I went to the office of Scott Perry, the general manager.

"You're burning lots of bridges in a contract year," he said.

"You brought me here to win, not lose. I want to play to win every game in my contract year."

"Okay, do whatever you want."

By January 2019, with Erdoğan now completely obsessed with me, every decision I made—especially regarding travel—was analyzed from the standpoint of personal security. After I came back from my near kidnapping in May 2017, the FBI gave me a button I could press at any time of day to dispatch agents to my location if I felt I was under threat, and told me that they would inform their local field offices in the U.S. to be on high alert whenever I traveled to their city. I never pressed it, but I did follow their advice to always tell someone where I was going whenever I left the house.

That month, the Knicks were scheduled to play a game against the Washington Wizards in London. I didn't want to get on the plane, because I feared I would be extradited or murdered by a Turkish hit squad. This all made sense, because I kept getting death threats online, like one that read, *You son of a bitch, you will never be able to leave America and go* to other countries, cause we'll be waiting to shoot you in the head. I hope I'll be worthy of this task, you mother----er. On another occasion, I visited a coffee shop and three hours later got an Instagram private message telling me exactly where I'd been. The team's security personnel had even warned me, "If you go, you can't leave your room or do any activities for the time you're in London."[7]

My teammates were also petrified about me going. As I continued to take on Erdoğan regardless of the cost, they believed that they—or their wives and kids—would become accidental casualties of my behavior. So they started avoiding me out of fear. They didn't want to ride in cars with me or on the players' bus, so during road games I started riding in the second bus with the trainers, equipment managers, and other staff. I didn't think anything would happen to us in America, but the other players couldn't be totally convinced. It frustrated me, but I wanted to be respectful and have a team-first attitude.

I had a talk with Coach Fizdale and the front office about whether I should go to London. I didn't want to let my teammates down by not playing, but the team's leadership concluded I was right to be worried, and would not be upset if I didn't go. Fortunately, my teammates also supported the decision, promising to win the game for me. Adam Silver, the NBA commissioner, also had my back, and promised his support for my views no matter what.

One person who did not support my decision was Hedo Türkoğlu, my former teammate on the national team, a basketball role model, and friend. Türkoğlu had sunk deeper and deeper into the pro-Erdoğan camp ever since our dinner with Mehmet Okur in 2014. When I said publicly that I didn't want to go to London because "there's a chance that I can get killed out there," Hedo fired back by calling me "irrational" and "delusional."[8] I was shocked—Hedo and I were on good terms, and if he had a problem with me, he knew he could talk to me one-on-one on the phone. He claimed that I couldn't go because I had passport and visa problems, and that my concerns were part of a "political smear campaign."[9] But this wasn't true, and I posted a picture of my travel documents on social media to show I had no issues.[10]

Around that time, ESPN did a short documentary that profiled both me and Hedo and our different views of the political situation in Turkey. After the filming wrapped up, one of the producers called me. "Don't tell anyone I'm telling you this," he began. "When Hedo did his interview, two guys were in the room prepping him on what to say. He didn't look comfortable. But he had to do it." It occurred to me that maybe Hedo, whom I had called Erdoğan's "lapdog" at one point, had gotten in over his head and the government was now pressuring him to do things he didn't want to, or he would lose lots of fans.

Aside from Hedo, the other Turks who played in the NBA—Ersan Ilyasova, Furkan Korkmaz, and Cedi Osman—were good guys, and friends. But as my beef with the regime become more intense, they refused to talk to me. They knew I would never do anything terroristic. The only thing I terrorize is the [basketball] rim, I tweeted on January 16, 2019.[11] But they were scared that they would become a target of Erdoğan's crackdown and so refused to engage. I even tried to talk to them with my jersey covering my mouth: "Hey, dude, what's up?" No response. I don't hold it against them. I was confident that once the political conditions were different, things would go back to normal. Unfortunately, I am still waiting for that day.

Before the trip, the Knicks, mindful that my activism was irritating corporate sponsors doing business in Turkey, warned me not to do any media. But, me being me, I couldn't keep quiet. On January 6, I went on the BBC, telling the British people, "It's sad, as I love Harry Potter, and wanted to come see all of London so badly, but I can't take the risk."[12] The Knicks were pissed, and I think my defiance (besides my anger at tanking) helped convince them to release me after the team returned from London. They didn't want this mess on their hands anymore. A Knicks beat reporter even told me he heard about something Knicks owner James Dolan had said: "Give Enes whatever he wants to get him out of here. Don't even negotiate with him about the money. Give him one hundred percent and release him immediately."

In the end, I know it was the right decision not to go to London. I heard that when the Knicks plane took off, the Turkish government issued an Interpol request for my arrest. This was just one instance of Turkey abusing its Interpol privileges—in one day in 2017, it uploaded a list of sixty thousand wanted "criminals." On the day the Knicks went to London, I happened to be in Times Square and saw the news ticking across a big screen informing the world that I was on the Interpol list. I (as well as the people next to me, gawking at me) was in shock. If I had gone to London and the British government had complied with this request, I could have been sent back to Turkey. Soon after, the State Department told me that I should not leave American soil until I become a U.S. citizen. As a result, I also didn't travel to Toronto while playing with the Portland Trail Blazers later that year.

My decision to criticize the Knicks for tanking cost me almost all my playing time. From January 11 to February 5, or 12 games, I played only 41 minutes total. I wanted the world to know that my benching was not a performance issue, so I kept discussing my unhappiness with the media. The fans, who were sick of seeing the Knicks be a laughingstock year after year, were on my side. Whenever we played at Madison Square Garden, they chanted, "We want Kanter!" I looked at Knicks owner James Dolan squirming as he heard the fans calling for me (who also happened to be his son's favorite player on the team). The team was embarrassed at the sight of the fans revolting over one of its best players not playing. Eventually the Knicks told me that they would either trade me or buy out my contract.

During one of my last games with the Knicks, I didn't even warm up. My bags were already packed, and I was ready to get out of there. But I couldn't leave without a memorable farewell to the city and the fans who had been nothing short of amazing. I told my teammate Mario Hezonja, "If Coach puts me in, I'll do something crazy."

"What will you do, run around naked?"

I kept my plan a secret.

Eventually Coach Fizdale decided to put me in during the third quarter, and the fans went nuts. Before play started, I went to center court, dropped to my hands and knees, and kissed the Knicks logo. I've never heard the Garden that loud.

The day before the trade deadline, team president Steve Mills, Perry, and Fizdale called me into Fizdale's office.

"You have one hour," Mills told me. "If you don't get traded, we'll waive you."

"Okay, cool." Whatever it took to get out of New York.

I kicked back and spread my arms across the couch and crossed my legs in a relaxed, European style. I scrolled my phone and chilled while they worked the phone trying to find a taker for me. Most teams probably knew that the Knicks would have no choice but to buy me out, the way I kept telling the press that they were trying to lose on purpose, so the Knicks didn't get any offers. After sixty minutes, I was a free man.

I look back fondly on my time in New York because of the fans and the bright lights of the city. I would have loved to retire there, but that wasn't God's plan for me.

For the next few days, I hung out in Chicago with my agent as we pondered where I should play out the rest of the season. Two teams were chasing me hard as a key contributor for a playoff run: the Lakers and the Trail Blazers. I wanted to go to LA because of a chance to play with LeBron James—the highest-IQ player I have ever seen on the basketball court. I also loved the weather and good vibes of Los Angeles. But my agent encouraged me to go to Portland because they were a much stronger team with a better chance of making the playoffs. I was sick of losing so much with the Knicks, so Portland it was.

Portland, Oregon, itself was a sketchy city with a lot of crime and drug activity, and I didn't even like to leave my house there. But the Trail Blazers are an outstanding organization, and the team I joined was first-rate as well. Damian Lillard was an NBA superstar whose leadership skills were as solid as his jump shot. C. J. McCollum, his running mate in the backcourt, could also shoot the lights out. For the last twenty-five games of the season, we really clicked. When starting center Jusuf Nurkic went down with a foot injury, I slid into the starting lineup and the team didn't miss a beat, finishing 53–29, good for fourth in the Western Conference.

It was such a blessing to go from playing zero minutes to competing on a team headed for the playoffs, and I had the Knicks to thank for it. I got some revenge on them by trolling them in an interview: "I want to start by thanking the Knicks for this opportunity. If not for them I wouldn't be here." Players around the league called and texted me to cool it, but I had too much fun doing it. And Knicks fans around the country still cheered me on whenever the Blazers came to town. They knew I'd been mistreated.

I started every game in the playoffs, and it was a run I'll never forget. For one thing, our first-round series had us playing the Thunder, now featuring All-NBA small forward Paul George, in addition to Russell Westbrook. During Game 3, my best friend (and former teammate) Steven Adams and I played major minutes against one another. We knew each other's game well from years of tangling in practice, and would always joke with each other about which one of us was the strongest player in the NBA. Now the laughter was over. We smashed into one another like cars at a demolition derby while chasing rebounds. On one possession, while competing for an offensive board, Steven dislocated my shoulder after hitting me as hard as he could. The pain was unbearable, but playing hurt is part of the game. Before Game 4, the team doctors gave me a painkiller shot so that I could play. Even though it helped a lot, Steven knew I was still aching. Even the best friendships in the NBA are put on hold once the game begins, so Steven mercilessly hit my shoulder on every offensive possession and then laughed about it to my face while I was on defense. But I couldn't be mad at my best friend—he was just doing what any NBA player would do to win in the playoffs.

In Game 5, with a chance to send the Thunder home for good and the score tied 115–115, Damian Lillard buried a 37-footer as time expired (the NBA three-point line is 23 feet, 9 inches at its longest distance from the basket). This shot, which gave Dame 50 points for the game, was perhaps the greatest buzzer beater in NBA history. When he turned around and waved to the Thunder bench after nailing the shot, it was the wildest moment I had in my entire NBA career. I've never been on the court for something that unbelievable, before or since. It was even sweeter because it meant Billy Donovan went home for the summer. It's a good thing Lillard hit that shot when he did, because my shoulder was still screaming in pain, and I don't think I could have played the rest of the series if he didn't end it then.

In the next round, we beat the Denver Nuggets in five games. As a competitor, it was a rush to face off against Nikola Jokic, one of the greatest centers of all time and a three-time league MVP. The series was during Ramadan. I woke up for suhoor every morning at 3:30 a.m., then played at night while fasting. My teammates encouraged me and hid their water bottles so I didn't feel tempted to drink. During a timeout, I broke my fast on the bench with fruit, a PB&J, and Gatorade. I played well, and we won the series. The respect of my teammates gave me more energy than any food could. Our defeat of the Nuggets set up a Western Conference Finals matchup with—who else—the Golden State Warriors. The Warriors were fresh off another championship from the year before, and still as lethal as ever. Some players are so talented that there is no game plan for them. Steph Curry was one of those players, and the Warriors exhausted every guard in the NBA by running him around the three-point line nonstop, making you work hard on defense. Even if you get a hand in his face, he can score anywhere from within 35 feet with ease. If you decide to let Steph score but shut everyone else down, good luck stopping Klay Thompson and Kevin Durant. The Warriors also had Andre Iguodala, an elite defensive player who could do everything, and Draymond Green, a defensive stopper in his own right who by this time was the most irritating trash talker in the NBA, and my least favorite player to play against. At the helm of all of them was Coach Steve Kerr, who put together genius game plans to use his stars' talents. As talented as our Blazers team was, we were no match for one of the most legendary teams in NBA history. They swept us 4–0, and I looked forward to another break before the start of the season.

Over the summer, I saw that I had a new Twitter follower: Colin Kaepernick, the talented NFL player who had been without a job for several years because of his refusal to stand for the national anthem before games. I admired his willingness to fight and sacrifice for what he believed in. I followed him back, and soon we started texting. We agreed to meet up, and he gave me a lot of ideas for how to use our platforms as athletes. "Never give up," he said. "Always go out there and speak loud. And don't trust the Players Association—they only care about money. Always remember: if there is no NBA, that means there is no Players Association. So do not trust them."[13] This meeting would have major relevance for my activism a few years later.

After my solid playoff run with the Trail Blazers the previous year, I knew I'd have some good options about where to play for the upcoming 2019–20 season. But with my career as an activist now well established, I was growing less concerned with the money I could make as an NBA player. As free agency began, I was strictly focused on going to the largest media market I could so that I could gain maximum coverage for my words to support my oppressed countrymen (and, increasingly, issues affecting America). On the first day of free agency, my agent, Mark, called me.

"We have two offers. One is from Boston, which is proposing two years and ten million. The other is from Portland. They're offering two years at fifteen million total, with a player option after the first year. We should take that."

I wasn't convinced. To me Boston was the only desirable option. The city had an international scene and a gigantic media market. It was also the brain of America, home to elite universities like Harvard and the Massachusetts Institute of Technology, as well as many others in the surrounding area. With those factors in play, it wasn't a hard decision.

"I don't want to go back to Portland. I'm picking Boston."

Mark was shocked. "I hope you're joking."

"No. Boston is the best place for me."

"Let me talk to Hank."

Mark begged Hank, my manager, to convince me to choose Portland. "This is the biggest mistake of his life!" I heard him yelling. I had just played so well there, and they were willing to talk about a long-term extension after the first year. Portland was giving us forty-five minutes to agree to terms.

"I don't even need the forty-five minutes," I said to Mark.

"You're crazy!" he screamed, his voice shaking. Mark was all about money, and I thought he'd drop me as a client if he knew my real motivations for wanting to go to Boston. I didn't want to give him any reason to think that my goals were about anything other than basketball. Hank also stood to make more money if I took the Portland deal. Neither of them would have understood my decision if I tried to explain it. I just kept insisting on Boston.

Within the hour, I was a Celtic.

As I settled into Boston, I prepared to take advantage of the city's many opportunities to keep raising awareness about Turkish issues and spreading my message of the importance of equality and freedom. After moving into my new home, I put pieces of paper all over the wall in my bedroom listing which media outlets to talk to, and where to give speeches about Turkey and politics in general. By this point, the Erdoğan regime was tracking everything I said in public. In one dangerous episode, they tried to silence me through intimidation.

In September 2019, Erdoğan's son-in-law Berat Albayrak, a minister in the Turkish government, had come to the U.S. to participate in meetings related to the annual UN General Assembly in New York. At one of those meetings, a friend of mine had recorded him complaining to Hulusi Akar, the minister of defense, "Enes is still playing in Boston. This is unacceptable. He's visiting a mosque in Boston and hundreds of people are lining up to take a picture with him. We gotta do something about that."

"We'll do whatever we can to stop it," another voice—almost certainly Akar's—said on the recording.

A few weeks later, my best friend on the Celtics, Tacko Fall, and I went to worship at the Islamic Society of Boston mosque after morning practice in training camp. The moment we walked in, people started taking pictures and asking for autographs—no problem. The imam who led us in prayers that day warmly received us. "Come more often," he said. "It will set a great example for young people."

As we walked outside, we saw two Turkish-looking guys with scowls on their faces lingering in front of the mosque. They looked a little thuggish, decked out in all-black athletic gear, and were seemingly waiting for us. One of them started to scream and yell at me: "You're a traitor and a terrorist. You're the worst human being on the planet!"

I told Tacko, "Just relax. All they're gonna do is curse and yell at us. They can't touch us or they will be in jail." Tacko later told me, "At first I thought they were fans, then I saw the hate on their face before they even opened their mouths."

As we tried to ignore it and wait for our Uber, the other attendees leaving the mosque came out. "Why are you yelling at Enes?" said one of them. I took out my phone and started recording everything to show people just how far Erdoğan can reach into America. Tacko was shaking, terrified that the situation was going to explode into violence. As our car pulled up and we got in, one of the pro-Erdoğan thugs gave me the middle finger.

I was shocked that even Erdoğan's foot soldiers would do this in front of a house of God. The video went viral, and the Celtics security team talked to both Tacko and me. They got the FBI involved, which promised to investigate further. "If you see a car following you over the next few weeks, it's us," an agent reassured me. They also promised to post a police car in front of my house whether I was there or not.

This episode was disruptive, but the real hurt came a day or two later. I guess Tacko told his mom what happened, because he told me, "I talked to my mom. She said I shouldn't hang out with you anymore because I could get hurt." This was a punch in the gut, because as best friends on the team and fellow Muslims, we studied the Quran before practice and prayed together. After a few months we stopped talking entirely. In time, all my other teammates also became too fearful to hang out with me. It was just another casualty in my fight for freedom and democracy in Turkey.

These years were very painful ones for me, but I was grateful to have so many members of the U.S. government supporting me, both Republicans and Democrats. The first time I met former president Bill Clinton, a good friend of mine invited me to a small dinner in New York he was hosting while I was with the Knicks. We had a good chat about human rights issues, and I thought it was amazing that a former president knew me and my story beforehand. Another time, I met him at his house in D.C. "Bring other people's stories to your platform, and tell the world what people are experiencing inside the Turkish jails to create empathy," Clinton said. That advice has been at the core of my communications strategy ever since.

After I started criticizing Erdoğan and his cronies when the corruption scandal broke in 2013, they started madly working a case against me and Gülen at the presidential level. One of President Obama's advisers told me that Erdoğan spent two hours in a meeting with Obama—one that was supposed to run twenty minutes—demanding extradition of me and Gülen. Obama told him that he couldn't deport any green card holder back without a lawful reason, but Erdoğan didn't give up. Eventually Obama had to touch him on the shoulder and tell him, "I've heard enough of this."

After Donald Trump was elected president in 2016, Erdoğan begged him too to send Gülen and me back to Turkey. But nothing ever happened. In 2023, I talked with someone from the White House who had also worked in the Trump administration. He said, "For the last seven years, the Turkish government hasn't sent one solid piece of evidence about whether Gülen or anyone who is affiliated with the Hizmet movement was involved in a coup attempt or not. The only thing they ever sent us were boxes full of pro-Erdoğan newspapers. One solid piece of evidence, and there's a good chance Trump would have extradited him back to Turkey. But nothing turned up, so the case is closed."

There are plenty of reasons to cast doubt on the Turkish government's explanation of the so-called coup of July 2016. In fact, it seems highly possible that it was a Turkish government "false flag" operation designed to consolidate the power of President Erdoğan. At least two sources connected to the CIA are skeptical of the Erdoğan government's official explanations.

In 2024, while at a political event, former CIA director and secretary of state Mike Pompeo walked in. I had built a minor relationship with him, beginning when we traded direct messages with each other a few times on X (formerly Twitter) while he was secretary of state. I was excited to see him, because of something he wrote in his book *Never Give an Inch*, released in 2023. I walked up to him and said, "Thank you for calling out Erdoğan in your book and calling what happened in Turkey in 2016 a 'purported coup.'" He shook my hand very tight, smiled for a second, looked into my eyes, and said, "No need to thank me. This is what I believe in."

In Pompeo's telling, "Turkey has every incentive to align firmly with the West as well as a population that welcomes it and benefits from it. Yet ever since a purported 'coup' in 2016, President Erdoğan had gone full Islamist-authoritarian. I spent countless hours with him and his national security advisor, Ibrahim Kalin, and intel chief, Hakan Fidan," Pompeo wrote in his book.

When Pompeo visited Turkey for the first time as CIA director in 2017, he said he was subjected to a lengthy video of the coup events, apparently prepared by the Erdoğan government as a propaganda piece to convince foreign visitors of its narrative regarding the events of July 15. Pompeo made another visit to Turkey in 2018 as secretary of state and then again in 2019, accompanying Vice President Mike Pence to persuade President Erdoğan to halt military intervention in Syria. During the visit, Erdoğan asked for "a few minutes" alone with Pence, but the meeting lasted much longer than expected. Pompeo described what happened next:

> *After about half an hour, I told our hosts that I needed to see the vice president. No dice. About twenty minutes went by, and now I was determined. Without permission, I walked down the hall and tried to push open the door of the room that Erdoğan and the vice president were meeting in. It was locked. I then told my counterpart that we were going to break through the door—I was worried that Vice President Pence was being subjected to the same three-hour video of the 2016 coup that I had been forced to watch on my first visit to Turkey as CIA Director in 2017. The video was so long and obnoxious that I considered it a mental health issue!*

Another challenge to the Turkish government's narrative came from an anonymous CIA operations officer who was in Turkey during the events of July 15. The interview was published in April 2024 on the website for the magazine *Homeland Security Today*.[14] The interview was conducted by Mahmut Cengiz, an associate professor and researcher with the Terrorism, Transnational Crime & Corruption Center and the Schar School of Policy and Government at George Mason University.

"The Turkish military is well trained, well experienced in coups, and has advanced weapons. It would not have closed just one way of the Bosphorus Bridge and done a coup," said the CIA officer, referring to the closure of one side of the bridge on the night of July 15. Court testimony from troops during coup trials revealed that soldiers were ordered to close one side of the bridge in response to a reported terrorist attack.

The CIA officer also found it perplexing to witness the Turkish government's swift removal of over ten thousand alleged members of the Gülen movement from various government institutions within just twelve hours of the alleged coup. "[Turkish officials] must explain how they could produce a long list of suspects" in such a short period of time, he said.

The purge following the alleged coup was not confined to the military but extended to the judiciary, police, intelligence agencies, academic institutions, and others. More than four thousand judges and prosecutors, including senior figures from the top appeals and constitutional courts, were immediately dismissed. This underscored the Erdoğan government's intent to influence the narrative in coup trials, transform the Turkish judiciary into a political tool under Erdoğan's control, and suppress opposition and dissent. Nearly two hundred media outlets were shuttered, hundreds of journalists were arrested or forced into exile, thousands of nongovernmental organizations were closed, and the wealth and assets of many businesses, totaling tens of billions of dollars, were seized and redistributed to Erdoğan's associates and supporters. According to a statement by Justice Minister Yılmaz Tunç to the state-run Anadolu news agency on July 12, 2024, a total of 705,172 people have faced legal action, primarily through detention and arrest, since July 2016. Among them, 125,456 were convicted on bogus charges related to terrorism and/or the coup attempt. The CIA officer noted that the Erdoğan government's attribution of the coup to the Gülen movement served multiple purposes, including discrediting Fethullah Gülen, who has distanced himself from the Erdoğan government and opposed its use of Islam for political objectives.

Regarding the failure of the Erdoğan government to secure the extradition of Gülen, who has been in self-exile in the U.S. since 1999, the CIA officer said, "From a legal standpoint, the Turkish government did not present the United States with any shred of legal evidence that proves Gülen was involved in the alleged coup attempt. Most of the documents presented would not stand a chance in any court of law. The documents were filled with emotional tirades and assumptions, which would not have been enough to indict Gülen, let alone extradited to Turkiye."

The officer confirmed the stance taken by the U.S. Department of Justice regarding Gülen's extradition. Despite repeated extradition requests and efforts by the Erdoğan government to secure Gülen's temporary detention in the U.S., American officials resisted these demands. The Justice Department concluded that the Turkish requests did not meet the legal standards for extradition set by the U.S.-Turkey extradition treaty and U.S. law. Therefore, extradition could not proceed without additional evidence substantiating the allegations against Gülen.

Similar skepticism about the so-called coup was also expressed by Turkey's other NATO allies. The German Federal Intelligence Service (BND) was unconvinced that Gülen was behind the failed coup in Turkey. "Turkey has tried to convince us of that at every level but so far it has not succeeded," Bruno Kahl, the head of the BND, said in an interview with *Der Spiegel* published in March 2017. In April 2017, German intelligence expert and author Erich Schmidt-Eenboom asserted that Erdoğan, not the Gülen movement, was behind the failed coup in Turkey, citing intelligence reports from the CIA and BND. Speaking during a program on German public broadcaster ZDF, Schmidt-Eenboom said: "According to CIA analyses, the so-called coup attempt was staged by Erdogan to prevent a real coup. The BND, CIA, and other Western intelligence services do not see the slightest evidence implicating Gülen in instigating the coup attempt."

In the words of the CIA operations officer interviewed in *Homeland Security Today* who evidently has a deep understanding of Turkey, Erdoğan benefited personally from the coup events but inflicted serious harm on Turkey as a whole. "The impact of the alleged coup attempt devastated Turkey's chances of meaningful collaboration with the European Union and solidified all negative impressions or assumptions about Erdogan and his regime. Erdogan may have benefited in the short term but hurt Turkiye in the long term. Turkish people are less free and more afraid, their future looks more uncertain, and the firing of judges only weakens the judicial system and the world's confidence in the Turkish government to afford its people any fair trials."

Besides Pompeo, one person who deserves my gratitude is Senator Ron Wyden of Oregon, a big Blazers fan. He stepped up to defend my rights in March 2019, writing to the State Department that "America cannot and must not stay silent in the face of such a blatant assault on free thought and expression," and urging that the U.S. government never cooperate with any Turkish extradition request against me.[15] I didn't fear extradition when I was inside the U.S., because the terms of the U.S.-Turkey extradition treaty require any offense to violate both Turkish and U.S. law, and I didn't even have a parking ticket in America. But I was still reassured knowing that people at the highest levels of government had my back, from presidents to cabinet secretaries to members of Congress. Other allies have included Senators Kevin Cramer, James Inhofe, James Lankford, Ed Markey, and Thom Tillis, and members of the House like Gus Bilirakis, Hakeem Jeffries, Kevin McCarthy, and Steve Scalise. I hope Americans who may be depressed by political battles know that many of our public officials on both sides of the aisle are still passionate about uniting to protect freedom and stand up to dictators.

CHAPTER 9

CHALLENGING CHINA

"My head wouldn't stop bleeding."

It was the night of August 31, 2019. Eighteen-year-old Joseph had just entered a subway station to make his way home, along with other citizens of Hong Kong who had just conducted a peaceful protest on behalf of their freedoms.

Then all hell broke loose.

A swarm of police officers entered the station, smashing their batons against the bodies of anyone who looked like they could have been a protester. Joseph instantly became a victim of this heartless repression. A police baton caught him on the top of the head, opening up a gash that required fourteen stitches to close.

That night, the police arrested Joseph, and he spent two days handcuffed to a hospital gurney without facing any charges. "I thought police brutality was something on the news or Facebook Live. I'd never imagined that would happen to me," he recalled.[1] Tragically, scenes like this were an everyday occurrence in Hong Kong throughout the summer of 2019, as millions of Hong Kong citizens rejected an assault on their liberty.

That year's fight for freedom would eventually trigger one of the greatest public relations crises in NBA history.

It would expose the league's double standards on human rights.

And it would trigger my fight to defend the freedom and dignity of all people oppressed by the Chinese government.

Ever since the United Kingdom ceded control of Hong Kong to China in 1997, the Chinese Communist Party (CCP) had ruled Hong Kong under a promise of "One Country, Two Systems." That meant that Hong Kongers could exercise the freedoms—including free speech—that China promised to it when Britain handed the city over.

But the CCP crossed a major red line in 2019. In May, the party introduced legislation that would make it easier for it to extradite Hong Kong citizens to the mainland. Every thinking resident of Hong Kong realized that the CCP was laying the groundwork to extradite any Hong Konger who defied the party. It made a mockery of One Country, Two Systems. In response to the assault on their freedom, throughout the summer of 2019 millions of Hong Kongers peacefully took to the streets in protest. The CCP routinely launched brutal crackdowns, fired rubber bullets, jailed protesters, and basically confirmed that it would now rule the territory with an iron fist.

This disgraceful episode was just the latest evidence of the Chinese Communist Party's freedom-hating core—and Americans knew it. U.S. politicians of both parties started speaking out and meeting with Hong Kong activists. Speaker of the House Nancy Pelosi tweeted, If America does not speak out for human rights in China because of commercial interests, we lose all moral authority to speak out elsewhere.[2] In October, Congress unanimously passed a bill requiring the federal government to sanction Chinese and Hong Kong officials committing human rights abuses.

But not everyone was so supportive of the Hong Kong democracy

IN THE NAME OF FREEDOM 133

movement. Chinese martial arts movie star Jackie Chan, a reliably pro-Beijing voice despite becoming wealthy and famous thanks to the American film industry, provoked the wrath of many Hong Kongers when he said the protests were "sad and depressing . . . safety, stability, and peace are just like fresh air, you never know how precious it is until you lose it."[3] In other words, he saw the protests as causing unnecessary chaos. The CCP no doubt loved this statement.

Even though Hong Kong's chief executive withdrew the extradition bill on September 4, the protests continued. October 1, the seventieth anniversary of CCP rule over China, saw some of the most explosive demonstrations yet, leading to many incidents of violence.

The world was watching. The NBA wished it wasn't.

On October 4, Daryl Morey, the general manager of the Houston Rockets, tweeted a symbol of protester support and the words "Fight for Freedom: Stand with Hong Kong." Morey was an analytics-obsessed team architect whose teams usually made the playoffs. He'd run the Rockets for twelve years and developed a reputation as a brilliant guy. Perhaps his thoughtfulness caused him to speak out about Hong Kong.

Either way, with one tweet, Daryl triggered a fight for his professional life.

Almost the entire NBA immediately had a meltdown over his tweet. The Chinese government asked NBA commissioner Adam Silver to fire him.[4] To his credit, Silver refused, but the pressure on the Rockets to throw Daryl overboard was enormous. ESPN reported that Joe Tsai, the Chinese-born owner of the New Jersey Nets (and the cofounder and chairman of Alibaba, China's version of Amazon), lobbied the NBA to fire Daryl.[5] Tsai also wrote an open letter to NBA fans on Facebook in which he called the Hong Kong protests a "separatist movement"—parroting language Beijing favors.[6] Rockets owner Tilman Fertitta tweeted, Listen . . . @dmorey does NOT speak for the @HoustonRockets.[7] Most people in NBA circles were far closer to Jackie Chan's perspective than Nancy Pelosi's.

Bizarrely, the NBA also put out two different statements for the American market and the Chinese market. "We recognize that the views expressed by Houston Rockets General Manager Daryl Morey have deeply offended many of our friends and fans in China, which is regrettable," said the first sentence of the statement in English targeting American fans. But the first sentence posted on Weibo, a Chinese site similar to X/Twitter, read, We feel greatly disappointed at Houston Rockets' GM Daryl Morey's inappropriate speech, which is regrettable.[8] In other words, the league was comfortable telling Chinese fans (and the Chinese government) that Daryl's opinion was dead wrong—demonstrating the opposite of support for the foundational American value of free speech.

What was strange about the NBA's reaction was that it had always been supportive of players and personnel whenever they spoke up for social justice causes. In 2012, LeBron James tweeted a photo of him and a Miami Heat teammate wearing hooded sweatshirts with the hashtag #WeWantJustice—a reference to the recently slain unarmed Black teenager Travon Martin, who was wearing a hoodie when he died.[9] No one in the league office had an issue with that. In 2017, Adam Silver announced that he was moving the All-Star Game from Charlotte to New Orleans because of legislation in the North Carolina legislature that the league viewed as anti-LGBT (the bill mandated bathroom usage based on biological sex).[10] And of course, many players, coaches, and even Adam Silver himself had encouraged me to be a champion for Turkish freedom.

The whole firestorm got me thinking: *This is weird. The NBA has always been supportive of me over what I believe with Turkey. They've supported other causes. Why is everyone going crazy over Daryl?*

A day later, my agent Mark called me. "China is watching your Twitter very closely," he said. I'm not sure how he knew that. Maybe someone in China was worried I'd say something and threatened the NBA, which passed the message to Mark. Or maybe the NBA took its own initiative to say something based on my Turkey-related activities on Twitter. In any case, I was stunned to hear this.

"What? Why?"

"Because you are always criticizing Turkey, they think you will be the only one to say something about Hong Kong and China. Don't say a word."

Mark always had my back on my fight against the Erdoğan regime, even if he didn't understand why I was doing it. Why was he urging me to stay quiet?

The next day, I figured it out.

At my very next practice with the Celtics, an assistant general manager came down to the floor. In our team huddle, he sternly warned us all, "Listen, what Daryl Morey tweeted made a huge mess. We're going to lose millions. Do *not* say a word about it."

It was then that I realized that it was about the money. With the NBA, it's always about the money.

To his credit, my coach, Brad Stevens, pushed back on the assistant GM. "The guys can say whatever they want. They just have to be prepared for the consequences."

Little did I know at that point just how many consequences I would face.

Prior to this point, I had never given a thought to the relationship between the NBA and China. But I soon began to learn just how much money the NBA and its teams make in China from broadcasting games, selling merchandise, and holding exhibition games. Daryl's tweet threatened to end all those revenue streams, which then combined brought in about $4 billion per year.[11] Why? Because the Chinese Communist Party basically bribes its critics into silence. If you criticize China, its government, or the country's lack of freedom, the CCP will prevent you from making money there. This is why you never see Hollywood movies in which the bad guys are Chinese—China will prevent the movie from being released in China, costing the studios millions. During the COVID-19 pandemic, when the Australian government demanded that the Chinese government properly investigate the origins of COVID, the CCP retaliated by imposing economic damage on Australia through tariffs on Aussie wool and wine. The list goes on and on.

Sure enough, in response to Morey's tweet, China extorted the NBA in a similar way. The Chinese Basketball Association suspended its cooperation with the Rockets, as did Chinese apparel company Li-Ning. Rockets games became invisible on Chinese TV. China canceled a G-League exhibition game with a Rockets affiliate. It would be a financial gut punch for the league if it suddenly vanished from China altogether.

The fact that Daryl, the general manager of the Houston Rockets, had spoken out was especially painful for the league. The Rockets were the most popular NBA team in China because of Yao Ming, China's version of Shaquille O'Neal. Seven-foot-six Yao's entrance into the NBA in 2002 as the top overall pick was a cultural phenomenon, and an undeniable symbol of the growing ties between the U.S. and China at that point in history. Yao ultimately played his entire career in Houston, averaging 19 points per game and making eight All-Star teams before retiring because of repeated foot injuries. In the process, he became a national hero in China and single-handedly did more than anyone in the world to make basketball extremely popular in his home country. The Chinese Basketball Association, which Yao chaired, slammed Daryl's "inappropriate comment" and announced it was suspending "exchanges and cooperation" with the Rockets.[12] This was a big deal.

Something unusual happened to me personally in the days after Daryl put out his original tweet: the media didn't talk to me for two or three days straight. This was not the norm—usually reporters asked to talk to me several times per week about Turkey-related topics and normal basketball things. But I hadn't gotten a single request for comment during one of the biggest controversies the NBA had faced in years. Strange, but whatever. More on this later.

Meanwhile, China continued to pressure the league to get rid of Morey, or at least have him renounce his views. The Chinese consulate in

Houston, for example, demanded that the team "clarify and immediately correct the mistakes." Eventually Daryl deleted the tweet and issued a half apology: "I did not intend my tweet to cause any offense to Rockets fans and friends of mine in China. I was merely voicing one thought, based on one interpretation, of one complicated event. I have had a lot of opportunity since that tweet to hear and consider other perspectives."[13] Numerous people on both sides of the political aisle criticized this outcome—Daryl seemed to have been bullied into saying sorry. That level of agreement indicated that millions of Americans were disgusted by the NBA's hypocrisy and worship of Chinese money. A headline in *Rolling Stone* put it well: "The NBA Chooses China's Money Over Hong Kong's Human Rights." To me, this result was immoral and insane. To almost everyone else affiliated with the NBA, it was just business. Adam Silver estimated that the NBA lost $400 million in Chinese business because of the effects of Daryl's tweet.[14]

On October 14, LeBron James chastised Daryl in an interview, saying he was "misinformed" and "wasn't educated on the situation at hand." LeBron added, "I do not believe there was any consideration for the consequences and ramifications of the tweet."[15] This was nauseating. The "consequences and ramifications" LeBron was referring to was money. In other words, LeBron was suggesting that Morey ignorantly expressed his opinion in a way that could hit the league in the pocketbook. I couldn't stand for LeBron's hypocrisy. For one thing, he had led his team to protest the killing of Trayvon Martin, so he should have had respect for political speech of any kind. Furthermore, on Dr. Martin Luther King Jr. Day in 2018, LeBron had tweeted a famous quote from the slain civil rights hero: "Injustice anywhere is a threat to justice everywhere."[16] Except in Hong Kong, I guess.

LeBron was known as the King, but I wasn't intimidated about calling him out publicly. I drafted a subtle response of my own on Twitter: Wow dude! A puking emoji followed as well. Then, in one of my most popular posts of 2019, I tweeted why we shouldn't take our freedom for granted:[17]

> Haven't seen or talked to my family 5 years
> Jailed my dad
> My siblings can't find jobs
> Revoked my passport
> International arrest warrant
> My family can't leave the country
> Got Death Threats everyday
> Got attacked, harassed
> Tried to kidnap me in Indonesia
> FREEDOM IS NOT FREE

Soon after, I got a call from Mark, my agent: "If you want another contract, do not tweet about this! Don't say a word!" He also told me, "It's in your hands to make your career a fifteen-year career or be done in a couple more."

I decided not to go any further with it at the time. But it was a little hard to keep quiet. Every media outlet wanted me for an appearance, from MSNBC, to Fox, to CNN. They knew that I would probably have something provocative to say about this because of my willingness to condemn the Erdoğan dictatorship in Turkey. But the truth was that I didn't know nearly as much about the evils of the Chinese government back then as I do today. I just decided to get ready for the season.

A few weeks after the Morey tweet, the Celtics played our first game of the 2019–20 season against Philly. I injured my knee in that contest and was out for the next seven games. But once I came back, I clicked with my excellent cast of teammates, which included Jayson Tatum, Jaylen Brown, Kemba Walker, Gordon Hayward, and Marcus Smart. We had an outstanding year and were rolling toward an NBA Finals appearance.

Off the court, as I thought about what had happened with Daryl, I became increasingly disgusted with how the league had responded. I wanted to talk to Daryl himself about it, so I hit him up on Twitter: I support you.

He wrote me back: I appreciate it.

A few months later, right before the COVID pandemic shut down normal American life, I had the opportunity to speak at the Sloan Sports Analytics Conference, held at the Massachusetts Institute of Technology. The conference, which Daryl cofounded and cochaired, is usually about the role of statistical analysis in sports, but I had been invited to talk about human rights with Howard Beck of Bleacher Report. The conversation didn't touch on China, but I did continue to speak up for my fellow Turks: "There's no freedom. There's no freedom of speech. There's no freedom of expression. There's no democracy. There's no human rights. . . . Turkey's the number one country in the world with the most journalists in jail. . . . There's a thousand families out there with a situation worse than mine."

Afterward, Howard and I were hanging out in the greenroom after my interview. A guy I didn't recognize walked up to me.

"Daryl Morey would like to speak with you," he said.

"Great, how about he comes here?" I replied.

"No, he wants to meet with you somewhere private. Follow me."

Daryl's staffer led me through a maze of hallways to a backstage area that was pitch-black. It looked like a movie scene for some secret meeting. Daryl and I couldn't see each other too well, but we shared a hug and a handshake. I think he chose such a hidden location because he didn't want anyone to see us and think that he was inciting me to speak up. Then, speaking in a low voice, he got serious:

"When I put out my tweet, I got so much pressure to take it down. Everyone was telling me, 'You're harming the league and people.' The NBA wanted to remove me from my position, but decided it wasn't worth the headache. I apologized, but they are still trying to push me out. When you put out that tweet about LeBron, everyone knew you were hinting at China, and it went viral. You didn't apologize. Be careful, because this could be the end for you. Don't trust whatever the NBA says. They want to make an example out of you."

The painful realization that my basketball dream could come to an end hung in the air like Vince Carter in his prime. But Daryl's splash of cold water in my face also came with a pep talk that has shaped my life ever since.

"Don't back down. No other athlete or celebrity is willing to talk about China like you are. You are the only one, so go one hundred percent."

I nodded quietly. *Someone has to do it,* I thought to myself. *If I'm the only one who can expose this whole system, then I guess I'm the one.*

Sometime later Daryl and I had another phone conversation. The message was the same: "Don't back down. You are the only one. Say what you're supposed to say."

I was getting ready. But then the world changed in a way nobody predicted.

On March 12, 2020, the Celtics were in Milwaukee to play the Bucks. All of a sudden, at breakfast, we received word that the NBA was postponing all its games because of the spread of COVID, which had first appeared in January. We boarded the plane to return home and the team told us, "Go home and don't leave your house. We'll call you and let you know what to do." All of us players thought the season was over for good. I went a little stir-crazy at home with a routine of cooking, eating, cleaning, and watching the news. But the time off also gave me plenty of time to read up on human rights issues.

More than four months later, the NBA season concluded inside "the bubble," a COVID-free environment at Walt Disney World near Orlando, Florida. The entire NBA universe—players, coaches, refs, and league officials—were now living inside a hotel and receiving COVID tests every day. Living on top of one another with no escape was hard. In the normal rhythms of an NBA season, players can go home and destress if they have a bad game or get mad at a coach or teammate. But there was no escape in the hotel besides being alone in your room. The lockdown rules were also strict: one player from the Kings who left the hotel to pick up Uber Eats was locked in his room for seven days. Fortunately, Steven Adams put it in perspective whenever I got too irritated by the situation: "You're living inside a five-star hotel at Disney World! This is not Syria. This is Florida!"

Although it was hard not to have the distance from the team we were accustomed to, it was also a blessing to get to know my teammates on a deeper level. Our coach, Brad Stevens, was largely responsible for this. After breakfast every morning, our team would watch film of the team we would play that night. Then Brad would lead the team in a conversation for about twenty minutes about life and adversity. He asked every player to tell a story no one knew about tough times that player had faced in his life.

These talks helped us grow as brothers. I learned a lot about teammates and the hard times many of them had growing up. One teammate said he grew up with no father and lived only with his mother. They were so poor that once, when their landlord evicted them from their house, he had to carry an inflatable mattress to sleep in people's yards for a while. When it was my turn, I told the team about how I had almost been kidnapped, and that my dad had been put in prison because of my outspokenness. We went way over the twenty-minute mark, and Brad had to break it up and order us into practice. Stories like the ones I heard from my teammates stirred up my sense of empathy for suffering people, no matter how rich or poor the country they live in might be.

The thing I remember best about the bubble was how all the players were simmering with rage over the death of George Floyd, a Minneapolis Black man who died in a police choke hold in May 2020. In the days after it happened, I myself had joined protesters in Boston, chanting, "I can't breathe," and telling the crowd, "We are on the right side of history."[18] It was important to ensure that the police treated everyone equally.

Now, months later, this ugly tragedy—which also led to the eruption of Black Lives Matter protests—helped provoke a lot of conversations between me and my teammates. With nowhere to go and little to do, I hung out every night with Jaylen Brown and Tacko Fall talking about human rights and social justice, and Jaylen helped me understand why the American civil rights movement was so important: it allowed Black Americans to live out the promises embedded in the Constitution and Declaration of Independence. When I didn't hear hatred of America from Turks growing up, I had always heard America was perfect—the "shining city on a hill." But America's complicated history of race relations challenged those ideals. I still believed America was an amazing country and blessed with far more freedoms than places like China or Russia, and all Americans should be grateful for them. But America still had a lot of work to do in terms of fighting racism. The more progress America could make on that front, the more the world would see us setting the bar for respecting human rights.

As the summer in the bubble dragged on, nearly every single player, including me, went all out with displays of social justice because of what had happened to George Floyd: wearing Black Lives Matter T-shirts, writing slogans on their shoes, and kneeling during the national anthem. Just eight months or so after the Daryl Morey firestorm, the NBA claimed to be okay with all these expressions—and even supported them. The league formed the National Basketball Social Justice Coalition in partnership with the National Basketball Players Association and National Basketball Coaches Association, and permitted slogans like "Say Her Name," "I Can't Breathe," "Education Reform," and "Vote" to be painted on the court. I was supportive of these efforts, because I believed it was important to create change for social impact. But the fact that the same fervor did not surround issues related to China showed that the league's focus was very selective. The fact that the league controlled every word on the court or the uniforms meant that I would never be allowed to put something like "Free Hong Kong" on my jersey. Inside the locker room, some players turned extremely cynical about the NBA and the owners. "They don't really care about all this social justice stuff. They just want to keep the players who make the money happy," one said.

In August, after Milwaukee police shot a Black man wielding a knife named Jacob Blake, the Milwaukee Bucks refused to take the court for a playoff game. The players put out a statement reading, "We are calling for justice for Jacob Blake and demand for the officers to be held accountable."[19] The NBA, sensitive to the political moment, calmly bowed to the players and postponed the games.

This put all the other NBA players in a tough spot. Some of us felt that following the Bucks' lead was the right thing to do. But we also knew that if we refused to play, we weren't going to get paid. And we didn't know how long this was going to go on for. I personally thought playing was the right thing, because people tuning into the game would see the phrases on the jerseys and hear the commentators talking about why the Bucks had taken a stand. The more attention, the better. If we didn't play, it was just another forgettable story.

Two days after the Bucks decided not to suit up, and after other teams decided not to play either, the players held a massive, players-only meeting in the bubble to figure out a long-term plan. On the way to the meeting, I ran into my coach, Brad Stevens. "Where are you going?" he asked. I told him that the players were about to discuss their path forward. "Whatever you decide, we'll do it," Brad reassured me. "This is totally your decision." I thought Brad's support for our rights was amazing. I know not every coach or executive would have been so supportive.

The players-only meeting was a heated session. Everyone was mad at the Bucks because they had forced all the other players into a difficult choice of whether to follow them or not. Players were raising their voices, and Patrick Beverley and Michele Roberts (the executive director of the National Basketball Players Association) got in a heated shouting match. Giannis Antetokounmpo, the Bucks' star player, stood up and told us that this was a decision that the team had made right before the game, and that the Bucks didn't mean to put anyone in a bad spot. "If you want to follow us, keep going. But we aren't going to play until something is fixed."

Then LeBron chimed in with a weird remark: "I'll be okay if I don't get paid. But you guys think about you." Then he abruptly walked out. It wasn't leadership on the issue in either direction, and the players were all mad at his apparent selfishness. Nonetheless, every one of his teammates on the Lakers, except Dwight Howard, followed him out in solidarity. In the end, the players decided the best course of action was to delay the games for a few days.

In the Eastern Conference Finals, held that September, the Celtics played the Miami Heat. The experience in the bubble had thrown off our momentum, and we went down 3–1 in the series. After the game, the tension in the locker room over losing boiled over. Marcus Smart started yelling, "I'm the hardest-playing guy on this team! We have to play harder!" This motivational technique did not go over well with the other players. Jaylen Brown flipped a table and screamed, "I work hard too!" Those two started to go at it, and backup forward Semi Ojeleye and I had to break it up. Because we were in the bubble, this wasn't a real NBA locker room, so the media heard everything. At that moment I knew we were going to lose the series, because we had no unity. We did win the next game, but Miami finished us in six games.

This was a hugely disappointing ending to a season that began with so much promise. Simultaneously, the U.S. was in the depths of COVID, making the world even more bleak. Millions of people knew that China had, at a minimum, lied about what it knew about the virus and when. In the winter of 2019–20, the CCP chose to pretend everything was fine rather than admit that it had a catastrophic public health crisis on its hands. The CCP's silence and desperation to look competent led to millions of deaths, trillions of dollars in economic damage, and a generation of children who lost ground in school. The true deceitful nature of the Chinese government was on display. The world should never forget who was responsible. I certainly didn't.

At the end of that season, the Rockets and Daryl parted ways, despite him being the NBA Executive of the Year the year before and leading the Rockets to the playoffs nine times. Maybe the basketball relationship had run its course, since the Rockets never won a title. But I'm sure the Hong Kong controversy had something to do with it. Again, the hypocrisy showed: The NBA had just spent months affirming the players in their promotion of social justice through slogans on their shoes and jerseys. Now Daryl was out because he had created a PR headache based on his beliefs? What a joke.

Just before the next season started, the Celtics traded me back to the Trail Blazers. With COVID still gripping the country, it was perhaps my most miserable year in the league. Besides getting a swab jammed deep in my nose for a test twice per day, I hated playing in an empty arena with none of Portland's passionate fans in the stands. Portland also has some of the worst weather in the country, and the rain and darkness wore on me. I basically lived out of a hotel room all year.

The only good part was that I loved my teammates and Coach Terry Stotts, who was probably the best teacher of the game I ever played under. And it just so happened that I had the best game of my NBA career, when I grabbed 30 rebounds to go with 24 points against the Detroit Pistons on April 10, 2021. Those 30 boards in a game were a franchise record, and I was the first NBA player to snag 30 in a game since Kevin Love in 2010. We had a good team, even though we lost in the first round of the playoffs to the Denver Nuggets.

As well as I played that year, my true concentration wasn't on basketball. I couldn't let go of what the league had done to Daryl. Wasn't the league encouraging us to talk about social justice issues? I knew I needed to expand my outspokenness on human rights abuses beyond those happening in Turkey. But with no fans in the stands and less media attention on the league than usual because of COVID, I decided that this year was not the year to make some headlines. I stayed quiet and thought about a strategy for how I would use the upcoming season to continue to give a voice for those who had no voice in Turkey, China, and elsewhere.

After the season, I again told Hank and Mark that I wanted to go back to a big market, since I was planning for this year to be the biggest one yet for defending the importance of freedom and human rights. When free agency started, Chicago and a few small-market teams were options. Mark also told me that Philadelphia liked me, but that it would be hard for their ownership group to tolerate me and Daryl Morey (now running the Sixers) on the same team. Apparently, they feared we'd make too much trouble. Finally, Boston was again offering me a contract. It was a no-brainer to head back there, even for the one-year veteran's minimum salary.

That summer, something happened that dictated the future of my activism. By this time I was using my camps as a way to connect with kids on tolerance, freedom, and human rights. In some countries, and even U.S. congressional districts, the public officials I met with beforehand were concerned about radicalization stoked on TikTok and urged me to promote peaceful coexistence.

Sometimes Turkey tried to mess with my events. In 2019, officials from the Turkish consulate in New York lobbied the Islamic Center of Long Island to stop me from partnering with them, and even had their thugs call the mosque and tell them things like, "If you don't cancel your basketball camps with Enes, then we will make sure that none of the board members of this mosque are ever allowed to visit Turkey. And if you still don't cancel it, then we will come and protest in front of it. All the parents will be scared to send their kids to the mosque ever again. The decision is yours." I couldn't believe that the Turkish government would go to such extremes to stop children from enjoying a free basketball camp. Sadly, the mosque bowed down to pressure from the Turkish consulate in New York and canceled

IN THE NAME OF FREEDOM 147

the camp. Fortunately, Representative Kathleen Rice of New York helped us find a new location—the Island Garden courts in West Hempstead.

In July 2021 I was holding a basketball camp for kids with Congressman Hakeem Jeffries (today the House minority leader) in his New York district. After this camp, the kids lined up to take pictures as usual. As I smiled for a photo with one of them, his dad yelled out something very odd: "How can you call yourself a human rights activist when your Muslim brothers and sisters are being tortured and raped inside Chinese concentration camps?"

This caught me off guard—I had no idea what he was talking about. I was still smiling for the picture, but I quickly turned around and told the father, "I promise, I'll get back to you on this one." After the camp was over, I canceled the rest of my day and started "getting educated on the situation at hand," to use LeBron's words. I began to read about the atrocities the CCP had perpetrated against Uyghur Muslims imprisoned in concentration camps in the Xinjiang (East Turkestan) region of western China. Millions of them were in camps or under tight surveillance every day. The Chinese government did this under the pretense of fighting terrorism, destroying the Uyghurs' dignity and liberty in the process. China was also trying to erase their culture and Sinicize (make Chinese) their Islamic religion—mosques were being destroyed, children were being put in state-run brainwashing camps, and CCP officials were even staying in Uyghur homes to stop religious practices. One former detainee reported to Amnesty International:

> *Some people would disappear for several days. When they came back their bodies were scarred. . . . I know one, because her bed was next to me. She disappeared . . . [when she came back] her hands were swollen. . . . She said don't talk to me because there are cameras in the cell . . . [but she did talk later and said that] two police tortured her. She said she was beaten. They also beat her on the soles of her feet.*[20]

Another Uyghur woman told Amnesty:

I was terrified when I found out that I would be sent to a facility, because my neighbour, who was in her twenties, was at a camp, and she and I had a drink and she shared her secrets. She said she was raped and forced to have an abortion. . . . She told me that she said several Han people raped her, that "two held my hands, two held my legs and one raped me."

This cannot be true, I thought. *If it were, the whole world would be talking about it. Either people are truly scared of China and want to keep this quiet, or this is fake news.*

I called Hank and ordered him to find me a survivor of one of these camps. He did, and a few days later I met with a Uyghur woman named Tursunay Ziyawudun. Tursunay was twice taken into a detention and reeducation camp, in April 2017 and March 2018.[21] Through tears, she talked for an hour about the violence inflicted on her, including being kicked in the stomach during interrogations, to the point that she is today unable to have children. In another video, she said that three men "[d]id whatever evil their mind could think of, and they didn't spare any part of my body, biting me to the extent that it was disgusting to look at. They didn't just rape. They were barbaric . . . an electric baton . . . was pushed into my private parts and I was tormented with electric shocks." She described to me other horrifying acts of torture, forced sterilizations, forced abortions, gang rapes, and other horrors she witnessed.[22]

At the end of our talk, I told her, "You've got me. What can I do to help you?"

"Nothing."

"What do you mean? We did this for no reason?"

"No," she said. "I don't need your help. I live comfortably in America. You need to help the millions of Uyghurs getting tortured and raped every day."

That day I resolved that I would help the Uyghurs, no matter what it cost me. But I needed more information, so I got in touch with the Human Rights Foundation, telling them that I needed about a month's worth of training and resources. "Please put together a package of information for me," I requested.

They were excited that someone with my fame and platform was ready to become vocal on China, and they assigned a Taiwanese woman named Jen to routinely brief me on all things China in the month before the season started. I was staggered as I heard her go into detail about the egregious abuses of Uyghurs, Tibetans, Hong Kongers, Taiwanese, Falun Gong practitioners, Mongolians, and many other ethnic groups inside China. I also learned about organ harvesting, the sprawling Chinese government surveillance state, and China's "50 Cent Army": a legion of state-backed online trolls and disinformation artists who are each paid the equivalent of fifty cents per post. After meeting in person and talking on the phone for about a month and relentlessly studying at night, I had gotten a better handle on all things China-related, all so that I could tell their stories of suffering to the world.

The situation in China was even worse than I imagined. How could the NBA be okay with its players criticizing the very home nation in which they made millions of dollars, but tell them to shut up about the world's largest dictatorship committing mass human rights violations every day? The double standard made me so disappointed that the same people throughout the league who had taught me about American values, and encouraged me in my stand for freedom in Turkey, had abandoned them when it came to China.

Around the time the season tipped off, I had a conversation with Heather Walker, the Celtics' vice president for public relations, which set me on fire. We were talking about my activism and comments in the media in a friendly way when she let me in on a secret.

"Remember when no reporters wanted to talk to you two years ago, when the Daryl Morey stuff happened?"

"Of course."

She took a deep breath. "I'll tell you the truth. The president of the Celtics ordered us to keep you away from the media for a few days."

"How come?"

"Because they were afraid you would say something to make the situation with Daryl all worse."

I could not believe what I was hearing. The Celtics kept me from speaking to reporters after Daryl's tweet because they were afraid of me compromising their bottom line. They would have never told me to shut up if an African American had gotten shot by a police officer, or if I was denouncing the Taliban's treatment of women. It was during that time that I told myself, *I am going to learn. And then I am going to destroy the whole system.* The world needed to know that the NBA was in bed with a disgusting dictatorship.

Now set on fire to fight for freedom more than ever, I focused my attention on making a huge splash—something the whole world would see—on China's desecration of human rights, just as the season kicked off. Just as I had brought to light the sad fortunes of thousands of innocent Turks, I needed to fight for 1.4 billion Chinese who had no true voice or true freedom. A few weeks before the season started, I asked Jen, "How are we going to educate others, especially young people?"

"Only you have that answer," she responded. "It could be an interview, or tweets, or whatever. But you need to find something so powerful that people will talk about it for years to come, and can inspire every sports fan around the world."

For days as the season opener neared, I struggled to come up with the right idea to make a splash. One night I was at home in New York City. I was living near Times Square, which pours out light for blocks in every direction. I shut the curtains and sat down to think about how to tell the story.

That night I had a dream of me sitting in my house in Turkey as a kid, watching Lakers games. I was transported back to the nights when I was fascinated by the players' shoes, like Kobe's 2000 Crazy 1 design.

After watching the games and seeing the kicks, I would demand that my parents buy me Kobe's shoes.

Shoes!

When I woke up, I had my idea. Every young basketball viewer is fixated on shoes, so why not use mine to bring attention to human rights abuses in China?

After some more thinking, I decided I'd find artists around the world who'd been oppressed by their governments and ask them to depict their struggles and stories through a design on the shoes. Then I'd wear them on the court to catch the media's attention. This was exactly the type of powerful gesture that Jen urged me to figure out.

The only question: whether I was ready to pay the price for doing it.

CHAPTER 10

EXILE

It was the morning of the 2021–22 NBA regular season opener. I was nervous as hell—and not because it was the first game of the year. I didn't want airport security to see what I was bringing on board my team's charter flight to New York City.

Even as NBA players enjoy private air travel to get from game to game, we still have to abide by federal rules requiring us to be screened before getting on the plane. This included having our bags searched. Ordinarily I didn't mind these security checks, but I had something stashed in my suitcase that I didn't want anyone to see: a pair of custom-designed game shoes with "Free Tibet" written in black letters in front of orange flames. I knew that if one of the Celtics coaches or front-office personnel saw the design, they would probably demand that I not wear them on the court. That would blow up my carefully designed plan for bringing attention to Chinese human rights abuses.

With my heart pumping fast, I stepped out of the security line and went to use the bathroom at the private aviation facility. I waited for the line to die down so that I'd be the last one to get checked, with no one from the team around who might accidentally get a glimpse of my controversial kicks. Then, emerging from the bathroom, I was startled to bump into one of the Celtics' assistant general managers.

"Hey, Enes! Did you get screened yet?" he asked in a friendly tone.

"Oh . . . not yet," I murmured.

"Well, let's go."

We walked over to the conveyor belt together and prepared to have our bags examined. In a split second when the Celtics management official was distracted, I whispered to the security official, whom I knew well from seeing him every time we went to the airport, "Hey, man, do I have to open up my bag?"

"I have to screen everything, you know that."

"I get that. Look, I don't want to do anything bad. All I care about is not letting the guy behind me see what's in my bag."

The security guard looked skeptical.

"I promise you, I'll take you out to a Turkish dinner if you let me go," I offered.

He thought about it for a second and then said, "Okay. I trust you. I'll let you go this one time."

With my shoes still a secret, I exhaled and walked toward the plane, the anticipation of the publicity storm that was soon to be unleashed building with every step.

Shortly before the season began, I got the idea to express my political views about China on my shoes. I was hyped up about the attention it would generate, but I quickly realized there were a few potholes in the road. For one thing, I couldn't wear Nikes or any other shoes made in China. Human rights groups have alleged that some Nike shoes are made overseas by human beings working in slavery-like conditions. There is even reporting that Uyghur Muslims who have been uprooted from their homes and shipped to the city of Laixi have been forced into stitching together Nike Shox and Air Max shoes in a factory ringed by barbed wire.[1] I had to find a company that made sneakers in line with my ethical standards.

I told Hank about my shoe plan, and he thought it was the craziest thing in the world. He was also nervous about riding into battle against the biggest dictatorship in the world. But he complied. After some research, he found a company in Los Angeles called Vibram that makes shoes with fair labor, and I ordered dozens of pairs of plain white basketball shoes. At the same time, my friends at the Human Rights Foundation, who loved my idea, began to research politically minded artists around the world who could lend their expert skills to creating powerful designs. After we identified them, we started to make contact to discuss different aesthetic ideas. We asked them to sign a nondisclosure agreement swearing them to secrecy for the rest of their lives about the work. And I planned carefully on when I would wear each pair of shoes, hoping to coordinate each one's message with a city where it would have special meaning.

The other barrier to wearing my special shoes was the NBA rules on footwear. I thought the NBA might have a legitimate case against me for expressing my social justice views on my shoes. But then I remembered how, in the bubble during COVID, players were writing phrases like "I can't breathe" and "Breonna Taylor"—a Black woman whom Louisville police had mistakenly shot during a drug-related raid in 2020—on their sneakers. To me, the NBA should have been willing to allow me to condemn human slavery as loudly as it encouraged the players to shout Black Lives Matter. But it wasn't certain they would be okay with what I was about to do. I told Hank, my manager, "Make sure you research it in the NBA rulebook," which is about five hundred pages long. "You have three days. They're going to try and nail me."

After three days, Hank got back to me: "There's no rule against it," he said.

"Are you sure?"

"My eyes are blurry from reading the rulebook. I can barely open them. Trust me, there's no rule against it."

Next came a decision on which designs I would wear to kick off the season. Although the Uyghur issue was heavy on my heart during this time, I didn't want to put the spotlight on them during the first game of the season so that no one could claim that I was just a Muslim supporting other Muslims. The first game of the season would be on the road against the New York Knicks, and I knew that the city had a large Tibetan community. That got me fired up to send a message to speak up for their homeland and culture.

I'd first gotten interested in Tibetan issues through the Dalai Lama, who has always been a voice for peace in the world and denounced China's "cultural genocide" of the Tibetan people, whom China has lorded over since 1951. As I dug further into the Tibet issue, I read about more than one hundred Tibetan monks and nuns who since 2009 have lit themselves on fire as an act of protest against Chinese rule. I thought that was such an incredible statement of passion for making your voice heard. To this day, the Chinese government continues to ruthlessly stamp out the Tibetan people's native culture, which centers on Buddhism. That is why the Dalai Lama has lived in exile since 1959.

Tibetan issues were also a gateway to learning about Hong Kong, and then Taiwan, a territory that wants to live in peaceful independence from China. You could say learning about Tibet triggered a waterfall of knowledge about the Chinese Communist Party and its trail of destruction everywhere it goes, and the fact that most of the world just lets the party have its way without ever speaking up. I had to be a force for change and show the courage that I hoped would spark others to denounce China's many crimes against free people and human dignity.

After smuggling the shoes in my luggage to New York, I connected with the people who would most appreciate my Free Tibet statement on my shoes: the Tibetan community in New York City, whom the Human Rights Foundation had contacted beforehand to arrange an event. The

Tibetans were delighted to have me come and eagerly accepted my one condition: that they keep my appearance quiet—no videos, no social media—until game time the next day.

The night before the game, I visited a Tibetan cultural center in Queens, where hundreds of people turned out. I received a hero's welcome walking in the door—the last celebrity to really speak up on behalf of Tibetans was the actor Richard Gere, who then got blacklisted by Hollywood for defying the Chinese government. The hundreds of attendees happily placed their phones in a big bag for the evening so that no one would ruin my surprise planned for the next night by taking photos and videos and posting them online.

Soon the Tibetan Americans draped me with hundreds of the white ceremonial *khata* cloths, a gesture of friendship that often symbolizes a wish for a safe journey. They even presented me one on a small pillow which the Dalai Lama himself had once worn. Though very light in weight, their combined mass strained even my muscular neck. I also heard many stories of family members back home whom China had thrown in jail for some reason or another. After a meal of Tibetan *momos* (steamed dumplings) and butter tea, I took the mic and told them about my plan for the game the next night: "Tomorrow a lot is going to change. Whatever happens, know that I've got your back and I support you. And Tibet will be free one day." Hundreds of people had tears in their eyes as they eagerly awaited the world getting a glimpse of my sneakers proclaiming their right to live in freedom.

But we had to keep it quiet until then. At the end of the night, I reminded my Tibetan friends not to post anything from the evening on social media because I didn't want the Chinese government or the NBA to realize I was meeting with the Tibetan community. If they suspected I was about to do something big, then my plan would have been ruined right before the big day. Many Tibetans graciously complied with my request to put their phones away after their leader, who helped organize the event, told them no one was allowed to take pictures or videos or post anything until after tomorrow's games.

The next day, hours before game time, I posted a video in which I expanded on the Tibet issue. Wearing a T-shirt with "Free Tibet" on it, I called Chinese president Xi Jinping a "brutal dictator" and said, "Under the Chinese government's brutal rule, Tibetan peoples' basic rights and freedoms are nonexistent."[2] The Chinese government was furious and acted like I was hijacking the issue for my own gain. "It's despicable to use Tibet-related issues to get others' attention," a foreign ministry spokesperson said. All highlights of Celtics games were pulled off Chinese media. But I know that I did the right thing. The Dalai Lama's office released a statement that said, "We are thankful to Enes Kanter, NBA player for speaking in support of Tibet."[3] In a two-minute video message he summed up the existential threat faced by the Tibetans under Chinese communist rule. "Every word that he said is true."

Later, when we left the hotel for the game, unbeknownst to anyone I carried my special shoes in my bag. During warm-ups, I still wore black New Balance shoes so that no one would suspect anything, or intervene before the game began. As is customary in the NBA, twenty minutes before the game began, the team returned to our locker room for our final game planning and pep talks. I waited until everyone emptied out and then put my Free Tibet shoes on. It was too late for anyone to try to stop me.

Or so I thought.

Now back on the floor, after player introductions, literally one minute before the game started, the Celtics equipment guys approached me with a very unusual message: "The NBA called us to tell you to take your shoes off." I have no idea how they spotted my shoes so quickly, and I'm confident no other player in league history has ever heard such a thing from an equipment manager.

"Am I breaking the rules?"

"No, but your shoes have already gotten so much attention internationally that the NBA is already telling us to tell you to take them off. Please don't make it harder on us. Just go back and change your shoes."

"If I'm not breaking the rules, then I don't care, even if I do get fined."

"We're not talking about getting fined. We're talking about getting banned from the NBA."

I was beyond shocked at the idea that I could be banned just for standing up for innocent people. This was the perfect moment for me to take a stand. I was preparing to take my citizenship test, so I'd been studying the U.S. Constitution. I closed my eyes and thought to myself, *Okay, we have twenty-seven amendments, and the first one is freedom of speech.* To just "shut up and dribble" would betray everything America stood for.

I turned around to the equipment manager and barked at him: "No! I am not taking my shoes off!"

I laced up my sneakers and got ready to play. Unfortunately, I sat on the bench for the entire half. At halftime, in the locker room, the equipment guys came over to me and apologized for the situation. My teammates overheard it and figured something was wrong because of my shoes, but we didn't talk about the elephant in the room, not in the middle of the game. I didn't get an explanation from the coaches as to why I didn't play in the first half, but you don't have to be Albert Einstein to figure out why I rode the bench.

When I checked my phone at halftime, I saw thousands of notifications on my social media accounts—more than I'd ever had. I also saw a message from Hank, telling me that every broadcast of Celtics games had been suddenly shut down in China. I didn't play in the second half either. The game went into overtime, and during one of the time-outs, my teammate Jabari Parker gave me a hug and told me, "You don't deserve this, but keep doing what you're doing. This is bigger than yourself." Jabari is a smart guy who was able to understand why I wasn't seeing any action.

We eventually lost the game in overtime, and my teammates were confused why I didn't see a single minute of action. Some asked me if I was hurt, and others complained that they really needed me out there. One of them, who I think understood the real reason why I didn't play, came up to my locker and told me, "I love you, but you are freaking insane." I approached one of the assistant coaches and said, "You didn't play me at all?" He replied, "You were in the game plan. I don't know why you didn't play."

Despite riding the bench the whole game, I could see that the shoes were having an impact. Many Tibetans were in the stands holding up the Tibetan flag all four quarters, and some spelled out E-N-E-S-K-A-N-T-E-R with each person holding up a posterboard with a letter on it. *My life is bigger than basketball,* I told myself when I saw that flag. *I don't care what happens moving forward. This is the path I want to take.*

After the game, hundreds of media outlets wanted to interview me about my shoes. But I told Hank, who handled my media, to decline all of them. I didn't want my teammates to think that I was doing this for attention. But that didn't stop the media from talking about what they'd seen. ESPN, BBC, CNN, Fox, NBC, the *Wall Street Journal, New York Times,* and countless other outlets did stories on my sneakers. It was everything I was hoping to achieve.

Seeing people who treasured freedom as much as I did cheering me on was also an adrenaline rush that gave me a hunger to keep going. Garry Kasparov, the Russian champion chess player and human rights advocate, tweeted, Another bold stand by my friend @EnesKanter. Is it a coincidence that he sat on the bench against the Knicks tonight in double overtime? Or is the NBA's love of Chinese money more important than the rights of their players and China's victims?[4] (Today my handle is @EnesFreedom.)

Before the next game, at home against the Toronto Raptors, pressure started coming down on me, and not just from China. The National Basketball Players Association (NBPA) is supposed to defend the players' interests, which you would assume includes the right to free expression. Not with billions in China money on the line. A member of the union's leadership called me shortly before our matchup with the Toronto Raptors. "We just got a call from the NBA," he said. "They are pressuring us to tell you not to wear any shoes with the 'Free Tibet' message on them."

"Did I break the rules?" I asked him.

"No, but you know exactly what you did, and you cannot wear those shoes again."

Then they went a step further with a threat: "If you don't do what we say, we're going to change the rules on shoes for the entire league. We'll talk to the NBA about going back to the rule where all players have to wear white shoes at home and black on the road. And six hundred NBA players will have you to blame for it."

"Okay," I answered. "I'm not gonna wear my Free Tibet shoes ever again."

"Do you promise?" they asked.

"Yes, I never lie. I promise."

"Thank you for your understanding."

I hung up on them without saying another word. It was true that I wasn't going to wear the Free Tibet shoes. But I didn't say anything about what my next shoes would be.

To prepare the shoes for each game, I would text back and forth with each hired artist (I am keeping them anonymous to protect their identities). I'd tell them the concept I wanted on the Vibram sneakers, and they would tell me their ideas for how they wanted to paint it. I generally was okay with whatever they suggested—they were the ones with the creative gifts for bringing my ideas to life.

With the shoes ready, just as I did before the Knicks game, I served an appetizer before the main course before the Celtics played the Raptors in our home opener. I posted on my social media accounts: Heartless Dictator of China, XI JINPING and the Communist Party of China, I am calling you out in front of the whole world. Close down the SLAVE labour camps and free the UYGHUR people! Stop the GENOCIDE, now![5]

At game time, even with the tension with the basketball world mounting, I was excited to whack the hornet's nest again. Calling the Chinese dictatorship to account for its crimes was what really mattered, no matter what the consequences. That night I debuted a pair of shoes with a message about the cruelty the CCP is inflicting on Uyghur Muslims in

Xinjiang: "Stop genocide, torture, rape, slave labor. Free Uyghurs." The world noticed, and again by halftime my phone was flooded with more calls, texts, and tweets. Some were cheering me on, and others were warning me that I was setting myself up for the end of my career. Based on the fact that I played only five minutes in the whole game, and only because it was the home opener, it sure seemed like unemployment was a real possibility.

After the game, the NBPA, to which I paid thousands of dollars every month to protect my rights as a player, called me again, furious.

"You lied to me!" the representative yelled. "I can't trust you to tell the truth ever again!"

I gave them a short answer, then hung up the phone in their face: "I never lied to you. I never said I am not going to wear 'Free Uyghur' shoes. I just said I am not going to wear 'Free Tibet' shoes."

Click.

What was so sad about all this was the fact that the NBPA had encouraged all the social activism during the bubble, and backed me up 100 percent whenever I spoke out against Turkey. Now they were basically putting a price tag on human lives in China. I paid them thousands of dollars per year in dues. And they wouldn't support me? Disgusting.

It was after the second game that real mistreatment for my political views began. Before the third game, I was on the team bus talking to Eileen O'Malley, the Celtics' social media coordinator and a great friend. She let me in on a secret: "The NBA called every team we are scheduled to play. They said, 'Don't take picture of Enes or post them.'" This was a shock. Previously, I was everywhere on ads and social media. Now I was being canceled. In my mind, writing words of support for these groups on my sneakers wasn't any different than what my teammates had done to honor George Floyd or Breonna Taylor. It enraged me that the NBA was so pathetically trying to keep me out of the public eye, and it didn't even have the honesty to tell me to my face why.

Similarly, NBA camera crews always film guys as they walk from the team bus or the parking lot to the locker room. You can see players showing off wild fashion choices, or looking hard with their game face on. The fans love it. But after the first two games I didn't see the camera crew filming me like they always did.

I had my suspicions why this was, so I decided to run a little experiment—my scientist father would be proud! I decided to walk through the tunnel with Jaylen Brown, a great teammate who was one of my best friends on the Celtics. Not only that, but Jaylen was one of the biggest stars in the NBA. *No way they won't film Jaylen Brown, even if he's with me,* I thought.

Wrong. As soon as the camera guys saw Jaylen and me coming, they pointed their lenses straight at the ground. *Now I know there's something wrong*, I told myself.

The next day I asked one of them, "Why aren't you filming me?"

He looked a little sheepish. "The league's communications people told us not to film you." They also told other teams things like, "If you see any fans that support Enes, or that have any kind of sign or flag in their hands, don't get them on film." Apparently the NBA didn't even want such images to be even accidentally captured and posted on social media by teams, players, or fans.

That night we were in Houston, the place where so much of the exposure of the league's hypocrisy on China all began. I decided to go all out for this one, in part to send a message to the Rockets for what they did to Daryl, and in part because Houston has a huge Chinese population, many of whom were completely supportive of what I was doing based on support I saw in the stands and on social media. One of the Chinese dissident artists had produced an unforgettable, highly provocative design for this game's shoes. On the outside of each sneaker was a brick wall with the words "Free China"—one side in English and one in Chinese. The inside of the shoes had the world-famous scene from Beijing's Tiananmen Square in 1989, in which a single brave Chinese man blocks the path of a hulking Chinese tank deployed to gun down protesting students. Picture this scene on my shoes—except with the head of Winnie-the-Pooh as the turret of the tank. On the inside of the other sneaker, a cartoon version of me held a severed Winnie-the-Pooh head.

It shouldn't surprise you that the cartoon Winnie-the-Pooh and related images are banned in China. The dictator Xi Jinping looks just like him.

These shoes poured major gas onto the fire. I was thrilled to see hundreds of people, many of them Chinese Americans, holding banners ("Thank You Kanter," "Free Tibet"), waving flags, and cheering for me to get in the game. They inspired so many other fans to do the same in the stands for the rest of the season. Another reason why the pictures and filming of me had been banned hit me—the NBA didn't want to anger China by making it seem like they were promoting me. They wanted me invisible. That night, I also unleashed a tweet reinforcing the message of my shoes:

> XI JINPING and the Chinese Communist Party
> Someone has to teach you a lesson,
> I will NEVER apologize for speaking the truth.
> You can NOT buy me.
> You can NOT scare me.
> You can NOT silence me.
> Bring it on!!
> #FreedomShoes

As Daryl had encouraged me to do, if this really was the end of my NBA career, I wouldn't go down without a fight. The idea of losing my dream job suddenly wasn't bothering me that much. For one thing, losing that didn't compare to what I had lost from taking on Turkey: my family and friends. And after you've had literal death threats hurled at you, had your family persecuted, and been harassed and called a traitor in person, the loss of a job and money doesn't seem too extreme. In addition, the more I protested, and experienced support in the stands and on social media, the more I realized the world needed me. There was no going back now, and I was at peace with it.

Our next game was in Charlotte to play the Hornets, owned by none other than the greatest player in NBA history, Michael Jordan. No one did more to make the NBA a global product than Jordan. Jordan is also the international face of Nike basketball. His Air Jordans transformed the company from a small running-shoe producer to the best-selling footwear brand in the world. To put it another way, the NBA as we know it would not exist without Nike, and vice versa. Nike was also at that time the NBA's official supplier of uniforms, in a deal worth $1 billion.[6] Unfortunately, there is evidence that Uyghur Muslims working for next to nothing are embedded in Nike's supply chains. Either Jordan, everyone up and down the corporate ladder at Nike, and Nike wearers didn't know this, or they knew and didn't care.

I couldn't wait to debut the shoes I had cooked up for MJ. The only problem was that I didn't have them in hand as the clock ticked down toward game time.

Because I didn't want to travel with my custom shoes for fear that they would be confiscated during travel, I hired a local Charlotte artist to prepare the shoes for that night's game. Unfortunately, she was running behind schedule to come to my room to paint the shoes. I had to get clever to even get her up to my room once she arrived. Because of the number of death threats I was getting at that time because of my views on Turkey and China, I had a security officer posted near my hotel room door. I couldn't just have a girl come up to my room in the middle of the day—that would look suspicious (and improper). And I didn't know whether the guard would alert the team.

I quickly hatched a plan to get around all this. I set my phone as a private number and called the security guards. Using a disguised voice,

I told them to come to the lobby immediately: "We have a situation," I said. Just as the guard left his post by my room, I texted my artist friend to come up, and she made it inside undetected.

She entered carrying a bag filled with paint and brushes. She showed me her proposed design on an iPad and it looked great. "Do whatever you want," I told her, "but I'm playing in front of Michael Jordan tonight, so make sure the world never forgets it." After an hour, she had painted a highly provocative design on a pair of Jordan Air Concorde 11s: "hypocrite Nike," "modern day slavery," "no more excuses," and "made with slave labor," all with red paint designed to look like specks of blood. I absolutely loved them for the urgent message they would send to a company that was making billions off slave labor. "Don't touch it for an hour," she ordered me.

Those shoes were the most shocking pair yet, and this game would mark the true point of no return. When I took the floor that night, I didn't even care about the game (and I don't think most of the media did either). Every camera was focused downward on my feet. Before tip-off, I saw Jordan's face. He was staring straight ahead with a blank stare and his hand on his face. Once again I sat on the bench the entire game, not playing a single minute. But that did give me a chance to see and hear the many fans in the stands who had come out to support me. The motivation was only building.

Afterward, Jaylen Brown told me, "I'll be honest. Have fun, and put it all out there, because you're never going to play after this year. If you keep criticizing Nike or China, you're done. So don't look back." Other teammates expressed similar thoughts. My agent, Mark, also called and made his final plea to me: "Look, I work for you. I don't work for the NBA, but I have to be honest with you. I am getting so many calls from all over the world. If you say another word, you are never going to dribble a basketball on an NBA court ever again. You're only twenty-nine years old, so you're throwing away another five or six years and forty or fifty million dollars. The choice is yours."

No problem, I told myself. *I'm going to go all out and expose the system.* I wasn't taking any media requests at this time, because I still didn't want my teammates to think that I was doing it for attention. Besides, it was clear that the shoes were speaking for themselves, and my social media postings amplified their impact. After the game, I fired off a tweet:

> To the owner of
>
> @Nike
>
> Phil Knight How about I book plane tickets for us and let's fly to China together. We can try to visit these SLAVE labor camps and you can see it with your own eyes.
>
> @KingJames
>
> @Jumpman23
>
> you guys are welcome to come too.
>
> #EndUyghurForcedLabor

My campaign continued to boil in the media afterward. In the days after the Charlotte game, CNN wrote that "NBA star Enes Kanter has doubled-down on his criticism of China and has called on Nike to do more in fighting against injustice in the country."[7] Bloomberg, *Sports Illustrated*, and the *Daily Mail* also ran stories. On Reddit, where someone posted a picture of the Uyghur shoes, the comments were overwhelmingly positive. "He is a legend," said one. Another user wrote, "I dig a lot of the Nike sneakers, but ever since learning about the forced Uighur laborers it really made me rethink about what companies I spend my money on."

With each passing day, I wanted to expose this hypocritical system more and more. It was nothing short of painful that many of the same people who had initially supported my activism on Turkey were now telling me to stay quiet. One of them was Colin Kaepernick, who three years earlier had given me encouragement to never quit. Despite being blackballed from the NFL, Colin still had a deal with Nike, and it was his top source of income. As soon as I showed my custom shoes to the world, he stopped contacting me. Ironically, Colin was right when he told me years ago not to trust the Players Association for support. Sadly, now I couldn't trust him either. He too was standing for social justice—until it hit him in the wallet.

Around the fifth or sixth game of not playing, I had a conversation with Coach Ime Udoka, who had replaced Brad Stevens that year, about why I wasn't seeing the court. "I know what you're thinking, but it's got nothing to do with your stance on China," he said.

"Okay, but you're losing games because of lack of rebounding," I said. "So I should be playing."

He had no answer for me.

Other than Jaylen, who quietly gave me encouragement to keep going, my teammates were mostly just confused as to what I was doing.

"I'm trying to expose all the evils that China is doing," I said. "There are so many injustices happening, and we need to speak up about them. That's what everyone was doing in the bubble."

"Okay," they basically said. "But educate us: What's a Uyghur, what's a Tibetan?"

One day at the practice facility I sat down with all my teammates for over an hour. They asked me questions about everything related to China, human rights, and my activism. At the end one got up and said, "What you're doing is amazing. Your shoes are the most inspirational ever created. We will support you, but not out loud."

"What do you mean?" I asked.

"We have shoe deals, jersey sales, and other endorsement deals. And we all want another NBA contract. So we can't risk it."

I asked them one simple question: "If your mother or sister or daughter was in one of those concentration camps getting raped and tortured, would you still pick money over your principles?"

Many of them turned around and left the locker room without saying anything after I asked that question. I was grateful to have the private backing of my teammates, but it was disappointing to know that they too prioritized their financial future over doing what was right publicly. In a way I was sympathetic, because they had families that depended on them. Heck, some of them were taking care of whole neighborhoods in which they grew up. But it broke my heart that I had sacrificed so much more than money in my own stand for freedom, and they couldn't raise their voice to defend the American values that allowed them to make such a good living. Ultimately I resigned myself to the reality that my teammates were never going to join me publicly.

After the Jordan game, my phone was blowing up with calls, texts, and social media messages. Fox News commentator Kennedy tweeted, @EnesKanter (@EnesFreedom today) is the bravest person in sports for reasons other fake activists could never fathom.[8] **Nathan Law, one of the leaders of the Hong Kong democracy movement, said,** We need more public figures like @EnesKanter to speak up against genocide and human rights violations.[9] With collective actions, we can make a difference." Most touching were the words of ordinary people, like an ethnic Uyghur who tweeted, As an Uyghur living with unimaginable pain and sorrow, hoping and praying day and night to wake the nightmares my people have been going through, We finally see the light that there are still people who have decency, justice and courage. Thank you, thank you for your support!!![10] **But the haters (quite possibly Chinese online trolls) came out too:** Enes Kanter is no more an expert on China than I am on geology, **said one account.** He's doing this for the fame, for publicity, and for the state. If he had ever been to Xinjiang, like I have, he would know it is easier to visit a mosque and practice Islam in China than to do so in the West.[11] **Whatever.**

With people making up reasons for my advocacy, I wanted to talk to Commissioner Adam Silver to make sure he knew that I was simply using my freedom to raise awareness about people being oppressed by dictators. When I requested a phone call with him through the NBPA, they gave me a flat-out no. "We're out," they said.

"But I'm not breaking any rules. Show me the rule that says I can't do this."

They then repeated the threat they had made earlier: "If you keep wearing the shoes, we're going to change the rules so that no messages are allowed at all. We'll go back to mandating black sneakers on the road and white at home."

"Fine," I told them. "I'll be the first one to follow the rules. But give me Adam's number."

They refused.

The day after the Charlotte game, I told Jaylen, who was the vice president of the NBPA, that they weren't being helpful. "I want to talk to Silver," I told him. "Can you do something?"

"You created the biggest mess since the COVID lockdown. Everyone is nervous about what you will do next. But you're my bro and I'll help you." It would have been incredibly damaging for Jaylen if it came out that he was supporting me, because he would be opposing the position of the union he helped lead.

He then searched his phone and retrieved the commissioner's contact information. "Here's the number. Don't tell anyone I gave it to you." He said this just above a whisper so that no teammates or coaches knew it was him who gave me the number. He had me type it into my phone rather than share the contact from his phone to mine, because he was nervous about leaving a trail of evidence.

Up until this time, I had always been on good terms with Commissioner Silver. He'd had my back on my right to criticize Turkey and on my refusal to travel to London out of personal safety concerns. But once China entered the picture, he used none of his massive powers to defend me publicly. It was just more evidence that the league cared about social justice only until it hit the owners' wallets.

I texted Adam and asked for a call. He texted back that he'd be available in three days.

Around this time, on the advice of the Human Rights Foundation, I began creating a record of as many conversations as I could. They told me that things were going to get wild, and that I might face public accusations and lawsuits over my comments, so it was important to leave a trail of evidence about what was said in any context. So I diligently began to record calls, screenshot text messages, and preserve emails. For audio recordings, I had to exercise extreme legal caution, because in some U.S. states it is not legal to record a phone call without the other party's knowledge. Massachusetts, home to Boston, was one of those states.

Therefore, in the hours before my call with Adam, I took a car ride to neighboring Rhode Island, where the laws governing recordings are more relaxed. But I still had to factor in New York State, where the commissioner's office was. When Adam called at 7 p.m. I ignored it, then called him right back. Under New York law, the person doing the recording has to initiate the phone call.

We talked for thirty minutes, and while Adam was respectful, and at least clarified that there were no official rules to stop me from what I was doing, he also said some things I couldn't believe. For one thing, he admitted that it's a "different system in China." This was such a weak way of saying he knew that China was run by an authoritarian dictatorship that crushes anyone who doesn't bend the knee to the Chinese Community Party.

He also claimed that he didn't know for a fact that Celtics games were being canceled in China. I told him that there was a State Department report that included criticism of Tencent, a Chinese company, for blocking Celtics games after I criticized China's domination of Tibet. Adam just mumbled something and tried to change the conversation.

In total, the conversation made it crystal clear that from the players on up to the commissioner, the NBA's China money was just too important. "Whatever you need, call me," Adam offered as the call concluded. Yeah, right.

I also learned something interesting about that call after it ended. A well-sourced NBA reporter sent a message to Hank and told him that two lawyers were in the room with Adam during the call, which was put on speakerphone. After he hung up, the lawyers advised him not to get further involved, since things were going to get messier. They recommended that

Adam let me do whatever I want and try to close this chapter in league history as soon as possible.

If that was the league's perspective, then I had nothing to lose. It was truly time to go all in. That meant going toe to toe with the league's biggest star, and Nike's biggest pitchman, LeBron James.

Ever since I entered the league, I always had respect for LeBron. He did good work advocating for social justice and starting a school for disadvantaged kids. But I had never gotten over his unprincipled comment that Rockets general manager Daryl Morey "wasn't educated on the situation at hand" when he spoke out for freedom in Hong Kong. In my mind, LeBron was a hypocrite by taking millions from Nike but telling Daryl to pipe down. Even worse, LeBron had (appropriately) fired back at a Fox News host who told him to "shut up and dribble" when he started talking politics in 2018. How was he not basically telling Daryl to do the same thing?

I'd had enough. On November 18, 2021, I fired off a tweet directed at LeBron:

> Money over Morals for the "King."
>
> Sad & disgusting how these athletes pretend they care about social justice
>
> They really do "shut up & dribble" when Big Boss says so
>
> Did you educate yourself about the slave labor that made your shoes or is that not part of your research?[12]

The "Big Boss," of course, was China.

Accompanying the tweet were photos of my shoes, including one pair that featured a Winnie-the-Pooh (Xi Jinping) placing a crown on LeBron's head. When LeBron's Lakers came to play in Boston the next night, I laced up the sneakers to send the King a message in person. He didn't say anything to me on the court. Maybe his silence was an acknowledgment that he knew deep down that he had been wrong.

My shoe campaign produced some good progress. In January, ESPN wrote an article that examined some NBA players' relationships with shoes made in China.[13] Dwyane Wade wore kicks made by Chinese company Li-Ning, which human rights groups say has, like Nike, made shoes with forced labor. Even worse, as the article pointed out, Wade had tweeted during the George Floyd protests, If you don't stand for something, you'll fall for anything. Seventeen other NBA players wearing Chinese shoe brands included Jimmy Butler, Klay Thompson, and Andrew Wiggins. Did they know they were putting on their feet products made by people subject to some of the worst working conditions imaginable? None went on the record for the article. "It is such a sensitive topic," said one agent in the piece. "Nobody's going to talk about it." That attitude was part of the disgusting complicity in genocide that basically the entire league was okay with.

Ever since Turkey revoked my citizenship in 2015, I had basically been a man without a country—somewhere between a Turkish citizen and a U.S. green card holder. As time went on, I realized that America was the only logical place in the world to permanently call my home. Not only had I spent more than ten years falling in love with the place and its people, but it was (and still is) the only country in the world that best embodies the values of freedom and democracy. Fighting for people deprived of liberty had become my life's mission, and there was no other nation that gave me such an opportunity. Along the way, so many American citizens—teammates, journalists, politicians, and activists—joined with me.

So, in November 2021, I decided to become one of them. I decided to forevermore raise my voice as a United States citizen. America would not just be the place I lived. It would be my home.

After determining my eligibility to apply for citizenship, I arranged to take the test that every prospective citizen must pass. When my teammates asked if I had started studying, I was nonchalant about it. "I'll be fine," I assured them.

"Dude, are you kidding me?" one of them said. "They are going to ask you hard stuff that most Americans don't even know. We're going to have to quiz you every day," they demanded. My teammates then printed out the one hundred civics questions that U.S. Customs and Immigration Enforcement asks each applicant and kept a copy in the locker room. Over the next few weeks, whenever the guys got bored after practice or on the team plane, they would randomly ask me the questions on the list.

"Who was the first president?"

"Umm . . . I can't remember."

The punishment for my forgetfulness was running "suicides"—a series of full-blown sprints up and down the court. If we were on the plane, then I'd have to do push-ups at thirty thousand feet. But they also promised that if I aced the test, they would throw me a party. After the first five days, I got in excellent shape because I didn't know a single answer. For the next few weeks, I studied day and night.

When I went in for the test at a federal building in Boston a few weeks later, a very nice woman sat in front of me and fired the questions off one by one. With every question I had a flashback to me running the excruciating suicides—an experience I absolutely did not want to repeat. Fortunately, I got every single one right.

At the conclusion of the test, the woman, a Celtics fan, smiled, gave me a big hug, and told me, "Congratulations, you're now an American!" It was the greatest day of my life. I was overjoyed that I finally had a country again, and to be able to be part of the magic of America: the fact that we are united as Americans, and not as distinct ethnic groups living inside the same borders. As President Ronald Reagan once observed, "You can live in Germany, Turkey, or Japan, but you can't become a German, a Turk, or a Japanese. But anyone, from any corner of the earth, can come live in America and become an American."[14]

Then the woman offered me something surprising: "Here are the papers if you want to change your name."

Change my name?

In about five seconds, I thought about how much I had sacrificed in the name of freedom, and how much opportunity America had given me. *I don't want to disrespect my family's name*, I thought. *But I want to make a statement about what I live for.* So I made Kanter my middle name and decided—on the spur of the moment—to change my last name to Freedom. I told the woman what I wanted to do, and her eyes started to water. Then I texted my teammates that I had passed my test, and they all responded by posting American flag emojis in the chat.

The next morning I went into the locker room, and the whole thing was decked out in red, white, and blue. The party my teammates had promised was underway. Grant Williams brought his own homemade cupcakes, taking care that they were prepared with halal ingredients. Before the next game, I walked into the locker room as usual, and was speechless to see that the equipment staff had already changed my jersey to put my new last name, FREEDOM, on the back. Before we took the court that night, our team broke the huddle with a chant of "One-two-three Freedom!" It was even more special because I knew my NBA days were numbered at this point.

When I checked in, the Boston fans gave me a standing ovation. After I scored my first points, the announcer screamed "Freedom!" and tears came to my eyes as I started running back on defense. My whole life flashed before my eyes, realizing that everything that I had been through had been leading up to this moment. It was in God's plan all along for me to fight for freedom as an American, and to do it in, of all places, Boston, the birthplace of the American Revolution, the so-called Cradle of Liberty. Best of all, I knew that even if the NBA and the players wanted me to shut up, the roar of the crowd confirmed that ordinary American citizens were behind me. That night, and in the days to come, I felt so blessed to be in a situation with total freedom of speech, expression, and religion. If things had gone differently, I might have become one of the nearly 13,000 Turks convicted of the crime of insulting the president from 2014 to 2021. But here I was, in the land of the free and the home of the brave.[15]

A few days later, on November 28, the Celtics traveled to Toronto to play the Raptors. With a fresh American passport in hand, the fear of being assaulted or kidnapped that had prevented me from traveling to Canada was obliterated. When our team plane landed in Canada and my feet hit the ground, I smiled. *This is what freedom feels like,* I thought. *I'll never have to worry about getting deported back to Turkey ever again.*

Perhaps the most humbling part of the experience of becoming a citizen came a few days later. I sorted through my fan mail at the practice facility to see a letter from former president George W. Bush. I couldn't even believe that he knew who I was. "Congratulations on becoming a United States citizen," he wrote in part. "America is a great land of freedom and opportunity. We are blessed by the diversity of our citizens, and encourage you to embrace this chance to add to our country's proud heritage."[16]

I absolutely will, Mr. President.

The pressure continued to mount on me throughout the season as I wore my shoes and kept speaking out for freedom. In late 2021 and early 2022, I publicly called for a boycott of the 2022 Winter Olympics in Beijing. "I feel like all the athletes out there need to go out and say, 'I cannot play a game where there is a genocide happening, where there is all the human rights abuses, where there is people getting tortured and raped in concentration camps,'" I told the BBC.[17] But whether it was athletes or International Olympic Committee officials, everyone gave me the same answer about why they were participating: "I have a family to feed." Nevertheless, I said, "[The IOC is] part of the problem because China doesn't respect human rights, friendship or freedom of expression. Shame on the IOC, organizing Olympic Games in a country like China." Florida congressman Michael Waltz and I also cut an ad together shining light on how corporate America was sponsoring what we called "the Genocide Games."[18] At the end, we had a simple message: "If it's made in China, put it down."

Around the same time, Yao Ming was asked at a press conference about my activism. Yao is the most famous Chinese athlete in the world. Unfortunately, he is also a tool of the Chinese Communist Party. "If there is an opportunity, I would like to invite him to visit China. . . . Then he may have a more comprehensive understanding of us," he said.[19] That sounded like a fair offer, and I accepted it, but I didn't want to be treated to some phony tour. "I want to say thank you to Mr. Yao Ming. . . . I actually do want to go to China and see everything with my own eyes," I told CNN. "But on this trip, I want to ask Mr. Yao Ming, will I be able to visit labor camps [in Xinjiang]?" I never got an answer, and he blocked me on Instagram. What an embarrassment for an otherwise admirable man and basketball hero to many. Sadly, the Olympics went ahead as normal.

Whether because of my shoes, my tweets, or my stance on the Olympics, my playing time remained inconsistent as the season dragged on—I would play only a total of less than ten minutes in the first thirteen games. It was painful enough to suffer for my beliefs off the court. But to be deprived of the chance to play—the thing I loved more than anything else—was intolerable. Throughout the season, I repeatedly told Coach Ime Udoka, "I know you aren't playing me because of the shoes." He protested, but I knew the truth. "I don't care. You do what you have to do. I'm going to keep going." Taking the court at all became an increasingly special thing to savor, knowing that my voice was costing me my career. My awareness was growing that I'd soon never play in the best league in the world ever again. No team wanted a player who damaged its own financial interests.

On February 8, 2022—two days before that year's trade deadline—the Celtics played the Brooklyn Nets in Brooklyn. It was, as always, a treat to be back in New York. I didn't see any minutes during the first three quarters but kept praying to find a way to see the floor. Fortunately, we were blowing out the Nets on the way to a 35-point victory, and Coach Udoka decided to empty his bench in the fourth quarter. He called my name to start the final period, and I had an intuition that this was going to be my last game in the NBA. I played my heart out, even in a relatively meaningless situation, finishing with 7 points and 12 boards in all twelve minutes of the fourth quarter.

With a few seconds left in the game, I knew I needed one last shot. I was waiting in the corner while our point guard brought up the ball. He passed it to me, and I prepared to put up a jumper. *If this is going to be my last shot ever, then I'd better make it.* I stepped back behind the three-point line and let it fly. In the course of just a few seconds, I heard my teammates screaming and chanting my name—even they knew this was going to be my final shot in my final game.

Nailed it.

The bench erupted. I broke into a smile, but my heart was also breaking at the same time, knowing that it was time to say goodbye to NBA basketball.

Seconds later, the game was over. For the last time, all my teammates came and hugged me in the locker room. None squeezed me harder than Jaylen Brown, and I really got emotional at that, knowing that the ride of a lifetime in the NBA had come to an end. We all knew I'd be released or traded in the next day or so.

On February 10, ten minutes before the deadline, the Celtics traded me and a few other benchwarmers to—of all teams—the Houston Rockets, which has a stronger relationship with China than probably any other team in the league. I was promptly released from Houston's roster, and I suspect the rest of the league quietly cheered as the Rockets made an example out of me.

Three weeks later, Celtics games returned to Chinese television.

CHAPTER 11

IN MEMORY OF MUHAMMED FETHULLAH GÜLEN

Fethullah Gülen (1938–2024) As a scholar, writer, and poet, Gülen inspired several generations in Turkey and around the world, including Enes Kanter Freedom, to support secular education, dialogue, and promote peaceful coexistence throughout the world. "The true essence of humanity is a heart that yearns for peace and harmony. Service to humanity is the highest form of worship. The purpose of our creation is obvious: to reach our utmost goals of belief, knowledge, and spirituality; to reflect on the universe, humanity, and God, and thus prove our value as human beings."

While I was writing this book, the person who inspired me to become the man I am, the person who opened my eyes, mind, and heart, the person who told me to love everyone unconditionally, Muhammed Fethullah Gülen, passed away on October 20, 2024.

On that day I was in Houston with one of my best friends, Hakan Şükür, a soccer player who many believe is the best to ever come out of

Turkey. Hakan won a Golden Foot—a prestigious honor recognizing an extraordinary career—and many other awards. He also still owns the record for the fastest goal in World Cup history. I was in my room about to go to sleep when I saw the heartbreaking news of Gülen's passing online. At first I didn't believe it—I thought Erdoğan was using his trolls to create fake news. But then I saw a media outlet affiliated with the Hizmet movement reporting the same thing. I immediately ran to Hakan's room and started banging on his door.

"Who is it?" he demanded to know, completely startled.

"Please open the door!" I yelled.

The second Hakan took a look at my face, which had been drained of its color, he realized that something was terribly wrong.

"Mr. Gülen passed away," I sputtered with tears running down my cheeks.

Hakan was just as stunned as I was. I walked into his room and collapsed into a chair, with him facing me sitting on his bed. For hours we stared into space, speechless. Not wanting to accept that our beloved guide was gone, we didn't even call any of Gülen's students to confirm the news.

Eventually we summoned the courage to call one of his closest students who also served as his main caretaker. We asked if the news was true, and he confirmed that it was. At those words, the tears began to flow again for both Hakan and me.

Hours later, I booked a flight to Pennsylvania because I wanted to see Gülen with my own eyes. I still didn't want to believe that the news was true. When I arrived the next day, I took a car to the hospital where he had died, and his students let me into his room. To this day, I'm stunned that I didn't cry at the moment I laid hands on his lifeless body still lying in the bed. Right before I left the room, I held his hand and said my last goodbye to him: "I promise you that I'll continue to carry this torch and am never going to give up, ever."

As Gülen's core followers and I planned his funeral, we knew it would have to be a space big enough to accommodate his many adherents living in the U.S. Unfortunately, two different arenas canceled on us after the Turkish government discovered the site for his memorial and pressured the venues to cancel the services. We finally found a suitable place called Skylands Baseball Stadium in northern New Jersey, and twenty thousand people from all over the world traveled there to pay their respects and pray. Hours later, hundreds of people made their way to his grave site in Saylorsburg, Pennsylvania, to watch some of his students and me lay him to rest.

I want to recount much of Gülen's life in order to commemorate many of his good deeds and disprove many nasty rumors that have been told about him over the years. Gülen was born in 1938 and started his career in the city of Edirne, in northwest Turkey, as an imam and preacher at a small mosque. During the 1960s and '70s Turkey was facing major social problems such as poverty, political polarization, violent conflicts, lack of equal opportunity, and government discrimination against a large part of society. The conflict between the nationalist "right" and the socialist "left" during the 1960s and '70s was especially violent. During these years, street fights and gun battles claimed the lives of thousands of youth. Tensions existed between Turks and Kurds, practicing Muslims and nonreligious people, Sunnis and Alevis, Muslims and Christian and Jewish minorities, and so on.

Gülen started preaching at Üç Şerefeli Mosque, one of the monumental mosques in Edirne, western Turkey. Following his appointment to Kestanepazarı Mosque in Izmir in 1966, he quickly became popular as an eloquent and passionate speaker who touched a nerve among Turkish citizens grappling with the issues of the day. In contrast to many discriminatory and hateful interpretations of Islam propagated throughout the Middle East, Gülen provided a holistic understanding of Islam that embraced science, reason, and pluralism. He steered clear of partisan politics and scapegoating. His logical preaching style and passionate depiction of the life of the Prophet Muhammad (Peace be upon him) and his companions drew large audiences to his sermons. People came from all around the region to listen to him, and audiotape recordings of Gülen's sermons were among the top sellers in the country.

Gülen also had a unique personal touch. He did not simply give sermons at his mosque; he organized question-and-answer sessions on Friday evenings that were open to all, where anybody could ask any question. He also rented movie theaters to speak on popular topics at the intersections of religion, science, and society. He even visited cafés to speak to cafégoers—people who might not be attending a mosque regularly.

Apart from his sermons, Gülen promoted an educational agenda to address the country's top social problems: poverty, intolerance, and discrimination. He and the movement he initiated—Hizmet—started by providing scholarships to students and helping them with housing. In the course of their work, they realized that many students with talent lacked the necessary educational foundations to qualify for a good college, so they decided to offer free tutoring services to students from economically challenged neighborhoods to help prepare them for the national college entrance exam. Eventually, in the 1980s, the Hizmet movement started opening private, secular, nonsectarian grade schools, including the schools I attended in Van and Ankara. Finally, during the 2000s, the Hizmet movement established fifteen universities around the country. Unfortunately, all of these institutions in Turkey were either shut down or given to President Erdoğan's cronies during his campaign to punish Hizmet movement participants.

After the Soviet Union dissolved in 1991, Hizmet followers started opening schools in Central Asian countries with Turkic roots, such as Azerbaijan, Turkmenistan, and Kyrgyzstan. Then they went all around the world with the same vision of deploying education as the best solution for addressing social problems in the long run. In places like Afghanistan, Pakistan, and some parts of Nigeria, where girls have limited access to schools, Hizmet participants opened schools for girls. In places where there were ethnic or religious tensions among segments of the society, Hizmet participants would reach out to these segments and provide scholarships to students to build a diverse student body. Examples of such schools were in Macedonia in the Balkans, where children of Macedonian, Albanian, and Serbian families studied together; Bosnia, where the children of Muslim and Christian families studied together; and Zamboanga, Philippines, where children of Filipino Muslim and Christian families studied together.

Hizmet schools have some characteristics in common: They are places where young minds can be protected from toxic political ideologies, harmful substances, and violent gangs. They provide a safe learning environment where students learn to respect each other and empower themselves to become contributing citizens. They teach multiple languages, push students to excel in academic subjects, and encourage participation in science project competitions. (Even Erdoğan's sons attended a Hizmet-affiliated prep school because of the quality of education they provided.) Hizmet schools also respected the cultural and religious values of parents wherever they operated, a characteristic that has even attracted parents and students to Hizmet schools in places where there are no Turks or Muslims.

I have mentioned throughout this book that during my growing up in Turkey, I was influenced by a culture full of negative stereotypes, especially those about Christians, Jews, and the Western world. But stereotypes in Turkey are often, sadly, not limited to those seen as "outsiders." The polarization and intolerance I witnessed as a youth living in Turkey during the 2000s was a scaled-down version of the country's domestic polarization during the previous decades between Turks and Kurds, Muslims and non-Muslims, and so on. During the 1990s, an organization called the Journalists and Writers Foundation (JWF), of which Gülen was the honorary chairman, started a series of forums where intellectuals of all different ethnic, religious, and ideological backgrounds came together to find common ground for addressing the country's social issues. These meetings, similar to gatherings like the Aspen Institute in the U.S., were named "Abant Platform," after Lake Abant in the province of Bolu in

Turkey, where the first few meetings took place. Some years later, Hizmet devotees would establish Dunya TV, the first private TV channel broadcasting in the Kurdish language, breaking a longtime taboo in Turkish society.

Gülen and his friends also reached out to the leaders of Turkey's non-Muslim minorities and invited them to be part of an interfaith dialogue process. Patriarch Bartholomew of the Greek Orthodox Church, Archbishop Mesrob Mutafyan of the Armenian Church, and Turkey's chief rabbi, David Asseo, accepted these invitations and participated in interfaith events. Gülen's contribution to interfaith dialogue in Turkey was later recognized by a personal audience with the late pope John Paul II in 1998. Influenced by these events, the Turkish government's Directorate of Religious Affairs later established an Office of Interfaith Dialogue. At one academic symposium in Istanbul during the 2000s, a Hizmet participant sat next to Patriarch Bartholomew and asked him how he was doing. In return. the patriarch asked, "Are you one of Gülen's students? Because no one else would come and sit next to me."

Gülen's social advocacy was not limited to education and social dialogue. In the 1990s, his supporters started a TV channel called Samanyolu TV (*Samanyolu*, incidentally the same name as my high school, means "Milky Way" in Turkish). In 1999 a strong earthquake rattled the northwest of Turkey. Samanyolu TV—STV for short—started a program where viewers were asked to help the victims of the earthquake. Later the program expanded and began projects for helping other people in need. Hizmet participants who contributed to the relief efforts ended up establishing a humanitarian relief agency called Kimse Yok Mu?, meaning "Isn't Anybody Out There?" This organization ran many relief campaigns to bring assistance to victims of major disasters all around the world. And in Africa and Asia, Kimse Yok Mu? started long-term projects such as medical centers, water wells, and professional skill education programs. In 2017 I had the opportunity to contribute to the relief effort for the victims of Hurricane Harvey in the U.S., organized by U.S.-based Embrace Relief, another organization established by Gülen's backers.

During the 1990s, Gülen came to the U.S. multiple times for medical treatment for his cardiovascular disease and finally decided to settle there in 1999. After the 9/11 attacks and other terrorist acts of murder, Gülen was among the first to condemn the terrorists and urge Muslims to fight violent extremism. Today there are more than one hundred nonprofit organizations in the U.S. started by Hizmet participants. Although they have a broad range of activities, these groups all reflect the priorities of the Hizmet movement through their focus on education, dialogue, and humanitarian relief.

Even after Gülen settled in the U.S., the Hizmet movement continued to grow in Turkey. Throughout the 1990s and 2000s, Hizmet adherents supported Turkey's bid for membership in the European Union, with the hope of strengthening Turkish democracy, and voted for pro-EU parties. This vision of Hizmet overlapped with the goals of the Justice and Development Party (known as AKP in English) which came to power in 2002 by promising to make reforms to prepare Turkey for EU membership. At the head of the AKP at this time was the former mayor of Istanbul, Erdoğan. In the first several years of his rule, he stated that democracy, human rights, freedom, Turkey's economic development, and membership in the European Union were his priorities, along with ensuring peace and stability in the region. As a result, he received the support of a number of groups, including Kurds and Turkish liberals, American and European leaders, and the Hizmet movement. However, when it became evident that his rhetoric and actions began to diverge and his true intentions were questionable, many groups, including members of the Hizmet movement and pro-EU Turkish politicians, started to criticize Erdoğan. In 2006, Gülen even wrote a letter warning Erdoğan to uphold democracy and stay true to his promises.

Unfortunately, around 2011, after his third election victory, then–prime minister Erdoğan made a complete U-turn from his promises to the people and took an authoritarian path. In particular, in 2012 he asked Gülen to publicly support his bid for executive presidency. But Gülen refused, on the basis that the system Erdoğan proposed lacked checks and balances on the power of the president. When Gülen and the Hizmet movement withdrew their support, Erdoğan responded by shutting down all college prep centers in the country, some of which were run by Hizmet participants.

As said earlier, in 2013 a huge corruption probe involving Erdoğan's cabinet members became public. Erdoğan claimed it was an attempt by Gülen sympathizers to topple his government. He accused everyone involved in the investigation, police detectives, prosecutors and judges, and Hizmet movement participants who did not distance themselves from the movement, of being traitors. He declared the movement an enemy of the state and began a witch hunt. The so-called coup attempt of July 15, 2016, enabled Erdoğan to take persecution to the next level and target hundreds of thousands of people. In the years since, all institutional and social activities of Hizmet have been shut down. Over 600,000 people have been investigated, with nearly 100,000 sentenced. More than 30,000 people are currently in prison, including over 5,000 women. The persecution continues as we speak.

Outside Turkey, however, and especially in democratic countries such as the United States, the Hizmet movement continues to thrive. Although things might look bleak for Turkish democracy right now, I am confident that in the long run, all that Gülen stood for will triumph. The best way for me and all champions of freedom, tolerance, and coexistence to honor his memory is to see that triumph happen.

CHAPTER 12

FREEDOM'S FUTURE

Sorry, Mr. Freedom, we cannot give you full coverage. You have a very high-percentage chance of getting killed."

I thought it was a joke. But then I realized that the insurance company representative I was speaking with was being serious. Dead serious, maybe you could say.

It was February 2024 and I was trying to purchase life insurance for myself. I've had a clean bill of health my whole life. I've been a pro athlete, so I've always taken care of my body. I don't even drive a car, so there was little risk of me getting hurt that way. But as it turned out, the insurance company had assessed the risk of me dying in some kind of assassination attempt. I don't know how they calculated it—maybe they simply looked at my social media mentions.

Either way, it makes a point. My life today is not just about living. It is about surviving.

When the Celtics returned to Boston from Brooklyn, I didn't sleep a wink. I stayed up all night packing up my house because I knew I would be out of the league within days. The day I was released from the Rockets—my final moment in the NBA—not one teammate sent me a message. That hurt, especially because I regarded so many of them as brothers in the absence of having my family around. They were clearly scared I might mention their names publicly and thus jeopardize their financial well-being. It was a sad, quiet end to the dream I had chased so hard starting in Van approximately twenty years before.

Nevertheless, life goes on. On the day I was cut I already had my bags packed for my next stop in life: Washington, D.C. I had been invited to lunch with almost every Republican senator, each of whom was curious about what I had to say. They all heard my story of how I'd sacrificed almost everything in my life—including my career—for the sake of speaking the truth. Some of them were tearing up at the end of my remarks when I asked, "How can the biggest dictatorship in the world fire an American citizen from an American organization?" One senator stood up and replied, "We have no answer. But we want to do whatever we can to help you. This is your home now." It was the first time in months that I felt like anyone outside the human rights world had my back in the face of the Chinese campaign to cancel me.

A few days later, I received another reassurance that I was not alone in my fight. Thor Halvorssen, the head of the Human Rights Foundation, unexpectedly called me. He said, "I know you've been through a lot. But it looks like God is closing one door and opening another. I just got the news that you've been nominated for the Nobel Peace Prize."

At first I couldn't speak. This was a completely stunning development—the first good news I'd had in four or five months—that caused me to nearly break down in tears. I believed that God was rewarding me for my struggle on behalf of innocent people. I had new motivation to fight after such a disappointing ending to my NBA journey. Soon the invitations to speak around the world flooded in, as did awards from various organizations. To this day I have hundreds of pieces of hardware in my house, with no place to put them. In a way, having those awards is more satisfying than having any NBA championship ring. Life is so much bigger than basketball.

Still, I was only twenty-nine years old when the NBA decided it was done with me. I still had a lot of gas left in the tank and my body was feeling healthy. I still loved the game and wanted to keep playing. I kept working out with my brother Kerem, now living in the U.S. for several years, for months afterward to stay in shape. One day my agent, Mark, called and told me that Panathinaikos, a Greek team that is consistently one of the best in Europe, was expressing interest in me.

"What do you think?" he asked.

"I love them!" I told him.

"Great! Let's start talking."

Mark and I opened up a dialogue with the team to sign a deal. Even though both sides were hopeful of an agreement, there were a lot of questions that first had to be answered. One of them was playing time. But much more serious was the question of security. Greece is next to Turkey, making me vulnerable to a kidnapping or assassination attempt. I knew from the 2022 State Department human rights report that the Erdoğan regime has abducted more than one hundred people from other countries in the years since the 2016 alleged coup attempt, and I didn't want to be one of them.[1] Nonetheless, I agreed to the Panathinaikos general manager's suggestion that I travel to Greece to watch the team play. If I liked what I saw, he would let me start.

Then, a week before I was to depart, someone from the team called.

"Enes, you're a great player. But we just had a conversation with the front office, and this deal isn't going to happen. We can't guarantee your safety here. If something happens to you, the world will blame us for it. We are proud of you, but this won't be a fit. I'm sorry."

By now I was used to seeing a good basketball situation line up only for it to fall through. It had become a major theme of my life. I knew what it was to suffer defeat. But this disappointment was extra bitter. I was still young and could still perform at a high level. Now, it was clear, Europe was not an option.

Soon after that, a team from Taiwan expressed interest in me. They weren't looking to improve their team as much as they were looking to sell tickets with me—a vocal supporter of Taiwanese freedom—on the roster. I was already a hero there because of my China work, and the team pitched me on a visit. The president of Taiwan, Tsai Ing-wen, was willing to film a video of me shaking her hand. I would then speak in their parliament before I visited the team. I gave an interview about the opportunity, which exploded in popularity across Asia.

Of course, that meant the Chinese government now knew about my plans. One of their officials met with a Turkish friend of mine who lives in China. He told him, "If Enes goes to Taiwan to meet with the president, or to give a speech to parliament, or to play basketball, we will deport every Turkish person who is friends with him and opposed to Erdoğan back to Turkey." I couldn't believe they threatened me like this. If I went ahead with my career in Taiwan, about two hundred friends would be thrown out.

I was horribly conflicted about what to do. I wanted to play. I wanted to stand up for Taiwan. And I sure as hell didn't want to lie down because of a Chinese threat. American officials like Congressmen Rick Crawford and Chris Stewart, thinking the Chinese were bluffing, were urging me to follow through, while other politicians were warning me not to. In the end, all I could think about was my friends who might be deported or harmed by the Chinese, and I decided not to go. This is a horrific example of blackmail that is all too common from China. It's scary and infuriating to know that the CCP is willing to be cruel to people who aren't even involved in your work. Unfortunately the party is willing to make almost anyone a casualty in its fanatical desire for power.

Now my basketball career was truly over. I was at a loss for everything. I once again was punished for doing what's right—standing up for innocent people. But where my future was concerned, I was in a way at peace. I saw that my old skin had been completely shed. There was no other path but to be a human rights activist full-time. And I was excited about it.

Over the last three years, I've reflected a lot on my NBA years. All in all, it was an amazing run for a kid from eastern Turkey. The average NBA career lasts about four and a half years, but I made it eleven. I recognize that I had the great privilege of facing off against some of the best players of all time. When I first came into the league, it was still a place where big men went to war with each other every night. I loved playing against Ben Wallace because he was so physical, and it was a challenge to outwork him for rebounds. But the guy I really got hyped up to battle was Dwight Howard. I know that the best big men in the NBA today would have no chance if they went against the Dwight of fifteen years ago.

At the time I left the league, a new generation of stars had taken over from the guys who were kings of the court when I first broke in. Giannis Antetokounmpo was one of them. Giannis was one of the skinniest players in the league when he was first drafted in 2013, and I didn't take him seriously for the first couple of years. But I've never seen a guy who got so much bigger and better throughout the years. He is now probably the hardest player to guard, in part because of his strength, which I got a taste of in a game in 2018. After I stopped him from going to the rim, he gave me an elbow to the face that needed stitches, so I gave him one back. Soon we were up in each other's face, and I took a headbutt from him. Inexplicably, I was the one thrown out of the game, but he was allowed to stay in. Maybe Giannis got preferential treatment because of his MVP-level status.

There were also players I completely hated playing against. Draymond Green was one because of his incessant trash talking. Chris Paul was another, for the same reason. Chris thinks he's smarter than you (and he's probably right) and lets you know it. I always set my hardest screens against him because he was so annoying. As for me and my own trash talking,

I did it often at the beginning of my career. But as I got older, I started using the Tim Duncan technique of softening guys up.

I don't have many regrets on the court. I played hard and stuck around for a long time because I developed good footwork in the post on offense and chased rebounds on both ends of the floor harder than most other players. In this way I maximized the talent I was given—and I don't think anyone can ask for more than that. The only thing that really hurt was that I never won an NBA championship. Raising that trophy alongside my teammates always looked like the most incredible moment that could ever happen. I was really excited for my teammates on the Celtics when they won in 2024, and am still hoping that Damian Lillard and Russell Westbrook can win one before they retire.

The thing I miss most about the league is simply having fun with my teammates. I spent years hanging with people around my age on the road—playing jokes on each other, going out to dinner, and enjoying the money we earned. Now I spend lots of time attending formal meetings in the very serious world of human rights advocacy. I wear a jacket and tie to mingle with straightlaced politicians who are mostly in their fifties and sixties. It's not the same level of humor that is found in the world of pro athletes in their twenties who are concentrated on playing winning basketball and having fun.

The other hard part about leaving basketball was the lack of escape that being on the court provided. I used to be able to mentally shut down the stress of my life outside basketball whenever the ball started bouncing. Now the league and the commercial powers behind it took that from me too. I wake up many mornings to see notifications on my phone of who got kidnapped, whose family member is now in jail, or the latest death threat against me. Turkey pays students on campuses to take videos of me getting harassed by them so that they can be used as propaganda. All those stressors and more were in place before I was kicked out of the league, but now there is no escape from them. The news hits my mind in the morning and stays there all day. The sanctuary of the basketball court—where five guys leave their problems aside to play as one unit—is now totally gone.

The reality of making enemies of the regimes in Ankara and Beijing also shapes my life in concerning ways. Not long after I became a citizen, someone from the U.S. State Department sent me a message asking to meet. We sat down and had a long talk in D.C.

"So far you've talked about Turkey, China, Russia, North Korea, Iran, Venezuela, and lots of other issues," they said. "Different governments are going to try to hurt you in different ways, and we'd like to brief you on what they are."

I sighed. "Let's do it."

They began to read off their briefing paper: "With China, from now on you will be getting messages, phone calls, direct messages, etc., from the most beautiful girls in the world. Do not answer them; they are Chinese spies."

To this day, the fear of being the target of a spy lives in my head constantly. I don't know how to trust anyone who approaches me. Do they want to have a genuine conversation or are they out to get me as a Chinese spy?

The State Department briefer continued: "The Chinese troll army will come for you too. Do not back down, whatever you post. China is paying those accounts to hurl abuse and threats at you."

"What about Russia?" I asked.

"This doesn't apply to America or Europe, but anywhere else you travel in the world, only visit a restaurant once."

"Why?"

"Because they will follow you and try to poison you. So you don't want to let them know your habits. Don't eat or drink anything unless they open the bottle or the container of food in front of you, because it could be poisoned."

"And Iran?"

"Iran is a different story. They don't play around with women or poison. They will come to your door and shoot you."

This was not an exaggeration. In 2022 the U.S. Justice Department indicted a member of Iran's Islamic Revolutionary Guard Corps for hiring people inside the U.S. to kill former national security advisor John Bolton for $300,000. The indictment also mentioned the Iranian leader of the plot offering the killer another job for $1 million—widely believed to be a bounty on Secretary of State Mike Pompeo. In 2023 the Justice Department also charged three men in an Iran-backed murder-for-hire plot targeting Iranian journalist Masih Alinejad after a man was caught wandering her Brooklyn neighborhood with an assault rifle.

They went on: "North Korea doesn't have a lot of power, but they could hack your phone."

"What about Turkey?"

"We don't worry about Turkey too much. The most they can do inside the U.S. is pay students at universities to try and catch you saying something bad about Erdoğan and turn that into propaganda."

It was extremely ironic and disheartening to hear them say that they didn't really consider Turkey a threat, especially after I was nearly kidnapped several years before.

I worried about traveling outside the U.S. Where could I be assured of a high degree of safety? The State Department gave me a list of twenty-nine countries where they were confident I would be safe. Most of them were in Europe, but a few (such as Australia, Canada, Costa Rica, Japan, and New Zealand) were in other parts of the world. Sadly, wonderful places like South Korea, Taiwan, and most Eastern European countries weren't on the list. I hope I can get to them someday.

In the meantime, I keep fighting for human rights anywhere, no matter what it may cost me. So much of my work continues to revolve around China—the world's largest dictatorship. China's ultimate goal under the Chinese Community Party and its brutal dictator, Xi Jinping, is to replace America as the world's leading power. I predict there will be a big war one day between the two countries—maybe over Taiwan—and that whoever wins is going to take charge and whoever loses will be buried. Economically, the war has already started. We can only pray that it does not become a shooting war.

One thing that breaks my heart as a Muslim is the hypocrisy of Muslim nations on the Uyghur issue. Many of them, including Turkey, have assisted China in genocide and repression by extraditing Uyghurs back to China when the government demands it. Many Muslim leaders around the world talk a big game about being the *khalifa* ("leader" or "ruler") of Muslims in their nation and elsewhere, but when it comes to China they are silent. Many Muslims do not realize that China's support for the Palestinians is all for show and geopolitical advantage over the U.S. If the CCP really cared about the Muslim world, it would not have Uyghurs in camps. It would not be producing a Chinese-government-approved version of the Quran. It wouldn't be destroying mosques in the Xinjiang region. And it wouldn't have banned me across the entire Chinese internet.

Probably because of my social media posts about human rights violations against Uyghurs, Tibetans, Hong Kongers, Falun Gong practitioners, the Taiwanese people, and other groups, TikTok, at the time of this writing still owned by the Chinese company ByteDance, banned me from the platform. When the CEO of TikTok testified before Congress in March 2023, Representative August Pfluger of Texas asked if TikTok had blocked me. The CEO, Shou Zi Chew, denied it, even though Pfluger showed him a screenshot of my blocked account. Then, magically, my account was unbanned in the middle of the hearing, with the company later claiming that it made an error. Sure. Today I continue to post on TikTok to use China's own weapon for brainwashing America against itself.

When I played for the Celtics, Israel's consul general in Boston invited me to a Holocaust remembrance event. The world—and especially the Muslim world—can never learn enough about the atrocities perpetrated by the Nazis against Jews and many other people. At this event, a very old woman in a wheelchair approached me and said, "I've never seen a Jew this tall before."

"That's sweet of you to say," I told her. "But I'm Muslim."

"Then what are you doing here?"

"I'm here to learn."

This woman, who had to be at least ninety, began to cry. I learned she was a Holocaust survivor. I could only imagine the emotions she was feeling, since so many Muslims worldwide hate Jews. I decided I needed to keep working to reconcile Jews and Muslims in any way possible.

In 2021 I got the idea for what I decided to call a Peace Basketball Camp. I wanted to get lots of people from both sides of the Israel-Palestinian divide together around the game of basketball to create friendship and understanding. I wanted to hold the camp in Jerusalem, so I ran the idea by some officials in the U.S. They loved it. They also brought up an important security consideration: "As your plane passes through Turkish airspace, Turkey could ground it with a fake bomb threat. And they could pull everyone off the plane and arrest you." I was concerned that the idea would die before it even could be born. But then the officials reassured me: "We'll get in touch with the airline and make sure the plane goes around Turkish airspace."

Prior to the trip, I had gotten DMs from so many people on both sides of the Israeli-Palestinian divide. Threats included "You're not a true Muslim," and "We'll see you when you come to Jerusalem, be ready." But when I set foot in Jerusalem, I received the warmest, most genuine welcome from both Muslims and Jews. It made me mad to think of all the lies and myths about Jews I'd been fed as a child. At the beginning of the camp, the kids refused to shake hands with one another. But all the divisions of Jew versus Muslim, Israeli versus Palestinian melted away as the kids began to play with one another.

The best story involved a young Palestinian girl who could not have been over the age of ten. A coach pulled me aside and told me, "See this girl? She's Palestinian. When her family told her she would be going to a basketball camp with Enes and Israeli kids, she said, 'No way.'" I purposefully put her on the same team with an Israeli boy wearing a kippah.

When he passed her the ball on offense, she scored a basket. Then she high-fived him when they were running back on defense. I think that moment was the highlight of my basketball career. At the end of camp, she was exchanging numbers with the Israeli kids, and to this day they follow one another on Instagram.

A few months later, several cardinals of the Roman Catholic Church at the Vatican and I came up with a similar idea. We decided to bring Muslim, Jewish, and Catholic kids together to play basketball and then have a conversation about the different faiths. So we rented a gym next to the Vatican and had an amazing time. After the basketball portion of the event was over, we would visit a mosque, a church, or a synagogue. All the kids would ask different questions, and priests, imams, or rabbis would talk about the importance of coexisting peacefully. It was amazing to see barriers of ignorance crashing down and kids having a more mature understanding.

I was also privileged to meet Pope Francis on this trip. As he passed by me in a wheelchair, his eyes widened as he assessed my height. "How tall are you?"

"Over two meters." (I'm 6'10".)

"Stand up."

I did as he asked.

"Yes, you're very tall," he said quietly.

"Please pray for my country, Turkey," I asked of him. "Erdoğan is destroying my country."

"If you pray for me, I'll pray for you," he said quietly. I also told him that Fethullah Gülen sent along his greetings, and he smiled.

Sadly, my visit to the Vatican was ruined by—who else—the Turkish government. The night after my historic day with the basketball camp and meeting the pope in January 2023, I posted everything on social media. I think that triggered the Turkish government to put me on its most-wanted list, with a $500,000 bounty on my head. I was astonished. A few hours later, an FBI agent called me with a warning: "This bounty thing can get very dangerous. It could trigger criminals or even serial killers who would want the money. We cannot protect you outside of the U.S., so you need to take the first flight back to America right now."

That night, I reluctantly boarded a plane home. I was heartbroken because I had a lot of meetings scheduled for the next day with the Catholic cardinals. We planned to discuss how we can keep bringing kids of different races, backgrounds, and religions together to talk about the importance of coexistence. "Because of my platform, whenever I say something, it goes everywhere and the Turkish government hates that," I told the *New York Post* a few days later. "They're really sick of it, and they said 'enough is enough' and are doing whatever they can to shut me up." Now, almost every week, I check to see if Turkey has increased the bounty on my head yet.

I have also had the opportunity to engage with another religious leader who is one of my heroes: the Dalai Lama. We were able to have an incredible public dialogue in February 2022. What is so remarkable about him is the fact that years of bearing the burden of Chinese exile and oppression has not made him jaded nor dampened his hope for humanity. During our talk, he asked me about the T-shirt I was wearing, which was a plain black color with FREEDOM written in white letters. I told him that was my last name, and what everyone was fighting for. He told me, "I love that word." When I asked him for advice to young people, he responded, "The young generation is our future. They have the opportunity to change the world. They should cultivate open-mindedness. There needs to be a tangible transformation in how modern education is taught. Modern education should promote a sense of oneness. We have to live together in harmony on this planet." I also wanted to ask him something lighthearted, so I asked what his favorite sport was. Much to my surprise, he responded by throwing a fist in the air. I could hardly believe that boxing was the favorite sport of the man who was considered perhaps the most peaceful in the world!

With this in mind, over time, education through sports has increasingly become my passion. We must reach the youth and form their attitudes early if the world wants to bring people together in lasting harmony and eradicate old hatreds—especially in the Middle East. Ever since I was a kid in Turkey, I had always wanted to start a series of schools. In Van, my home city, I would sometimes see kids who were nine or ten years old not going to school like they should, because their parents just wanted them to work instead. This broke my heart, because every child should have a shot at a good education. I promised my mom back then that if I ever became rich, I would start a network of schools.

In late 2022, I launched the Enes Kanter Freedom Foundation, promising to create understanding through sports among kids of both Abrahamic and non-Abrahamic faiths. My goal is to create the biggest interfaith basketball academy in the world and create understanding among kids of every faith in the process. I am currently planning schools in Los Angeles and New Jersey inside the U.S. and in Australia, Berlin, Jerusalem, and the United Arab Emirates overseas, as well as many other countries in Europe. Every academy will be a place where sports serve as more than just games—they will be a bridge to understanding, friendship, and leadership. The Enes Kanter Freedom Foundation will offer a unique blend of athletic training and educational programs designed to empower youth from diverse backgrounds. Every dribble, pass, and goal is a step toward a more inclusive future.

One of the most important nations I am focusing on right now is Greece. Of course, Greeks and Turks do not have a friendly history toward one another. But the Greek government has been an excellent partner in inviting me to do camps there. One of the reasons is that Greece has been flooded with refugees from war-torn areas of the Middle East, like Syria and Iraq. In our camp held there, we reached more than one thousand kids in three days who came to study universal concepts of religious tolerance and then play basketball. Many of them arrived harboring anti-Semitic, anti-Western ideas. But at the end of camp, I could tell that many of them were thinking differently.

Even though the world is in a bad state, and there are many forces of hatred and oppression at play, I remain an optimist. I dream that one day I will be able to go back to Turkey. I am an American now, but I will never lose a passion for the country I love. I especially dream about playing for the national team again one day. I miss having that red flag on my chest and taking the court with my Turkish brothers. In the meantime, I am also focused on making America the best place it can be by working with people on both sides of the aisle. Even despite our problems, America's future is still bright because of how many Americans still care about protecting freedom, democracy, and our way of life. I'm one of them. And once America's polarization subsides, I would like to continue my work in elected office.

After all I've been through and sacrificed, I live with a lot of pain. My career and my family have been taken away. I receive death threats and abuse publicly and privately. I live with the possibility of my loved ones in Turkey disappearing, never to be heard from again. And if people can't hurt me, then they will hurt people close to me.

Yet in the middle of all this, I refuse to let go of joy. When I see the faces of the kids I help, or the victims of repression who are grateful for my work, I feed on their energy. I am reminded that all I've sacrificed to make this world better is worth it. I could be a volcano inside on any given day, but my enemies will never see me sweat. They rejoice when they see you struggling, and I will never give them that privilege. Joy is my secret motivation to keep fighting. I have given up everything to fight for everything, knowing that freedom is not free. The road ahead will continue to be long and hard, but it is the one I have never regretted taking in the name of freedom. To all my allies in this battle: Let's keep fighting together. I love you all from the bottom of my heart.

ACKNOWLEDGMENTS

Telling my whole story in one place—and not just in interviews or on social media—is a project that requires much more than my own effort. Countless people have been a part of making this book come to life, whether on the editorial side or as people who have supported me throughout my life.

I have always lived with a vision to live for others. These days my life is dedicated to bringing peace, love, justice, democracy, and freedom into people's lives. There are many people who hate me for this. Sometimes I have wished I could dedicate this book to a wife and children. But after losing my family in Turkey, I have never wanted to give my enemies a reason to hurt me again.

First, my family has always encouraged me and supported me through the peaks and valleys of life—thank you, Mom, Dad, Ahmet, Betül, and Kerem. My prayer is that we will all be together again someday.

My respected life mentor, Mr. Muhammed Fethullah Gülen, and the followers of the Hizmet movement helped show me the way of peace, tolerance, and respect for all people from an early age.

I would also like to thank Bediuzzaman Said Nursi, whose timeless works of Risale-i Nur have laid the foundation for the Hizmet movement, inspiring generations with their depth and vision. Your works continue to guide countless souls, including my own, toward faith, service, and purpose. For this enduring legacy, I am profoundly grateful.

I would like to thank all the people of my lovely country, Turkey (or as we spell it, Türkiye). My message to all Turks around the world is this: I am still a very proud Turk. I love our Turkish flag and Turkish nation. No matter what, you will always have the top place in my heart. To all the brave people of Türkiye: You are all my family. Until we meet again, I love you all from the bottom of my heart.

In 2022, I discovered that I am part Kurdish, which I am proud of. I would like to thank all the Kurdish people who have supported me from day one. I will continue to be your voice.

I was so blessed to have the support of so many NBA teams, cities, and fans. I would like to first thank the Utah Jazz for believing in me and drafting me when I was only a nineteen-year-old kid. Jazz fans are extraordinary, especially all the amazing Mormons who have been very kind to me from day one.

Second, I am grateful for the best and craziest folks in the NBA: the Oklahoma City Thunder fans and the state of Oklahoma. When I lost my family, you became my family. You gave me more than just basketball. That's why I call you "Okla-Home." I can't thank you enough.

New York was one of the best and wildest cities in which I played. It still gives me chills when I mention your name. Thank you for helping take my human rights work global and being given the honor to play in the best arena in the world, Madison Square Garden. Once a Knick, always a Knick.

Knowing yourself is the beginning of all wisdom, and it was in Portland that I truly found who I am as a person. The Trail Blazers helped

ACKNOWLEDGMENTS

me along my basketball and spiritual journey. Huge respect to the Blazers family and one of the most loyal fan bases in the NBA.

It was while playing for the legendary Boston Celtics that my human rights work became unstoppable. It couldn't have happened without help from Boston—the brain of America. What an honor to wear that Celtics jersey and play for the most legendary team in the NBA!

I lived a dream playing in the NBA, and teammates like Steven Adams, Jalen Brown, Russell Westbrook, and Tacko Fall made the ride even more fun. I must also give a huge thanks to the rest of my teammates, coaches, strength coaches, trainers, equipment managers, general managers, owners, presidents, marketing teams, video coordinators, scouts, dieticians, cooks, ball boys, and all the people behind the scenes. We will always be a huge family.

Many people helped prepare me to take my game to the NBA level. Thank you, Coach John Calipari, Tim Grover, Fatih Karali, Mustafa Derin, and many others.

To the University of Kentucky and all the Wildcat fans—it still breaks my heart that I never got to play for you and the great state of Kentucky. But I cannot thank you enough for educating me, for giving me a home on campus, and making me a part of your life forever, no matter what. Big Blue Nation forever!

I am proud to call my managers and agents my friends. Thank you, Max, Hank, and Mel.

The entire Barry family showed me abundant care at a time in my life when I sorely needed it. I can never properly repay you, but I was grateful for every moment you helped me.

Thank you to Mia Robertson and Paul Choix at Simon & Schuster for their careful reading and wise suggestions for how to bring the story to life even more powerfully.

Matt Carlini and the team at Javelin were total professionals in guiding me through the process of securing a publishing deal and writing a book.

David Wilezol was a fantastic writing partner who spent many hours helping me tell my story.

Finally, to all my supporters and fighters for freedom throughout the world—thank you for giving me strength to face enormous challenges every day. This is just the beginning of our journey together!

NOTES

CHAPTER 6: BIRTH OF AN ACTIVIST

1. Dave Feschuk, "NBA Players' Financial Security No Slam Dunk," *Toronto Star*, January 31, 2008, https://www.thestar.com/sports/basketball/nba-players-financial-security-no-slam-dunk/article_bee61109-652c-5594-94c9-1649535c15f7.html.

2. Tulin Daloglu, "Erdogan Boxed In by Syria," *Al-Monitor*, January 2013, http://www.al-monitor.com/pulse/originals/2013/01/erdogan-turkey-lakhdar-brahimi-syria-policy-failure.html.

3. Tim Arango, Sebnem Arsu, and Ceylan Yeginsu, "Turkey Expands Violent Reaction to Street Unrest," *New York Times*, June 16, 2013, https://www.nytimes.com/2013/06/17/world/europe/turkey.html.

CHAPTER 7: ERDOĞAN'S REVENGE

1. https://www.wsj.com/articles/the-oklahoma-city-thunders-halal-guys-1461869415.

2. "Kanter: 'After I Leave the Court, the Fight Begins,'" ESPN, May 20, 2019, https://www.espn.com/nba/story/_/id/26784150/kanter-leave-court-fight-begins.

3. "Controversy Looms as Gulen Follower Enes Kanter Left out of National Team," *Hürriyet Daily News*, 2015, https://www.hurriyetdailynews.com/controversy-looms-as-gulen-follower-enes-kanter-left-out-of-national-team-84460.

4. https://www.nytimes.com/2016/07/17/us/fethullah-gulen-turkey-coup-attempt.html.

5. "Fethullah Gülen Opens Doors and Speaks Out Against Accusations by Turkish President Tayyip Erdogan," *CBS News*, 2016, https://www.cbsnews.com/philadelphia/news/fethullah-gulen-opens-doors-and-speaks-out-against-accusations-by-turkish-president-tayyip-erdogan.

6. "NBA's FETO-Linked Star Kanter Faces Arrest Warrant," *Daily Sabah*, May 27, 2017, https://www.dailysabah.com/investigations/2017/05/27/nbas-feto-linked-star-kanter-faces-arrest-warrant.

7. https://anca.org/nba-star-disowned-by-family-for-supporting-fethullah-gulen.

8. https://www.youtube.com/watch?v=yQzfI2xC8ik.

9. https://ca.sports.yahoo.com/news/turkish-nba-star-back-u-turkey-cancels-passport-133241463--nba.html.

10. https://www.espn.com/nba/story/_/id/19472840/turkish-government-issues-arrest-warrant-enes-kanter-oklahoma-city-thunder-newspaper-reports.

11. https://www.youtube.com/watch?v=RzoXLsVF2yM.

12. https://www.dailysabah.com/investigations/2017/05/27/nbas-feto-linked-star-kanter-faces-arrest-warrant.

CHAPTER 8: STANDING ON PRINCIPLE

1. "Hoops Comes First, but Enes Kanter Will Keep Speaking His Mind," *Oklahoman*, September 17, 2017, https://www.oklahoman.com/story/sports/nba/thunder/2017/09/17/hoops-comes-first-but-enes-kanter-will-keep-speaking-his-mind/60574709007.

NOTES

2. https://www.oklahoman.com/story/sports/nba/thunder/2017/09/17/hoops-comes-first-but-enes-kanter-will-keep-speaking-his-mind/60574709007/.

3. Enes Kanter Strongly Backing Protests, Wanted to 'Take a Knee,'" North Jersey, October 4, 2017, https://www.northjersey.com/story/sports/nba/knicks/2017/10/04/enes-kanter-strongly-backing-protests-wanted-take-knee/732529001/.

4. Brian Lewis, "Enes Kanter Scoffs at Possibility of Turkish Prison," *New York Post*, December 20, 2017, https://nypost.com/2017/12/20/enes-kanter-scoffs-at-possibility-of-turkish-prison/.

5. Yaron Weitzman's X post, June 18, 2018, https://x.com/YaronWeitzman/status/1008715860570181632.

6. Zach Braziller, "Where Enes Kanter Stands after Heart-to-Heart with Knicks GM," *New York Post*, January 2, 2019, https://nypost.com/2019/01/02/where-enes-kanter-stands-after-heart-to-heart-with-knicks-gm/.

7. https://www.bbc.com/news/newsbeat-46775970.

8. Mark Woods, "Hedo Turkoglu Says Enes Kanter's Smear Campaign of Turkey Is 'Irrational,'" ESPN, January 1, 2019, https://www.espn.com/nba/story/_/id/25705352/hedo-turkoglu-says-enes-kanter-new-york-knicks-irrational-smear-campaign-turkey.

9. https://www.espn.com/nba/story/_/id/25705352/hedo-turkoglu-says-enes-kanter-new-york-knicks-irrational-smear-campaign-turkey.

10. Enes Kanter Freedom's X post, @EnesFreedom, January 8, 2019, https://twitter.com/EnesFreedom/status/1082358590281637888.

11. Enes Kanter Freedom's X post, @EnesFreedom, January 8, 2019, https://twitter.com/EnesFreedom/status/1085565362844897280?.

12. BBC News, "Enes Kanter: 'I don't feel safe in the UK,'" https://www.bbc.com/news/newsbeat-46775970.

13. SSAC20, "1:1 with Enes Kanter," YouTube video, 55:15, February 28, 2020, https://www.youtube.com/watch?v=kEkKlGIYOCs&t=1240s.

14. Mahmut Cengiz, "Former CIA Officer Slams Turkish Claims of U.S. Role in

2016 Coup Attempt as 'Amateurish and Baseless,'" *Homeland Security Today*, April 26, 2024, https://www.hstoday.us/featured/former-cia-officer-slams-turkish-claims-of-u-s-role-in-2016-coup-attempt-as-amateurish-and-baseless/.

15. Ron Wyden, "Letter to the NBA Regarding Enes Kanter's Release," U.S. Senate, accessed December 20, 2024, https://www.wyden.senate.gov/imo/media/doc/Kanter%20FINAL.pdf.

CHAPTER 9: CHALLENGING CHINA

1. AFP, "Hong Kong Protests One Year On: The Student," RFI, June 9, 2020, https://www.rfi.fr/en/wires/20200609-hong-kong-protests-one-year-student.

2. Nancy Pelosi (@SpeakerPelosi), X post, May 29, 2020, https://twitter.com/speakerpelosi/status/1266085197092737026.

3. Jackie Salo, "Jackie Chan Sparks Outrage Over Comments on Hong Kong Protests," *New York Post*, August 16, 2019, https://nypost.com/2019/08/16/jackie-chan-sparks-outrage-over-comments-on-hong-kong-protests/.

4. Adam Silver, "China Asked NBA to Fire Rockets' Daryl Morey," *Washington Post*, October 17, 2019, https://www.washingtonpost.com/sports/2019/10/17/adam-silver-says-china-asked-nba-fire-rockets-daryl-morey/.

5. Brian Windhorst, "Brooklyn Nets Owner Joe Tsai Faces NBA's Uneasy China Relationship," ESPN, April 13, 2022, https://www.espn.com/nba/story/_/id/33723055/brooklyn-nets-owner-joe-tsai-face-nba-uneasy-china-relationship.

6. Joe Tsai, Facebook post, October 9, 2019, https://www.facebook.com/joe.tsai.3781/posts/2653378931391524?ref=embed_post.

7. Marc Stein, "Rockets' Daryl Morey Ignites NBA Ruckus with China," *New York Times*, October 6, 2019, https://www.nytimes.com/2019/10/06/sports/daryl-morey-rockets-china.html.

8. Dan Wolken, "NBA-Backed Statements on China Differ in English and Chinese," *USA Today*, October 7, 2019, https://www.usatoday.com/story/sports/nba/2019/10/07/nba-china-statements-different-english-chinese/3898513002/.

9. Brian Windhorst, "Heat and Other NBA Players Wear Hoodies to Protest Trayvon Martin's Death," ESPN, March 23, 2012, https://www.espn.com/nba/truehoop/miamiheat/story/_/id/7728618/miami-heat-don-hoodies-response-death-teen-trayvon-martin.

10. Katherine Peralta, "NBA Commissioner Defends Stance on North Carolina Bathroom Bill," *Charlotte Observer*, April 13, 2016, https://www.charlotteobserver.com/news/business/article73086142.html.

11. "Chinese Basketball Body Halts Cooperation with Houston Rockets over Offending Tweet," Reuters, October 7, 2019, https://www.reuters.com/article/us-china-basketball-nba/chinese-basketball-body-halts-cooperation-with-houston-rockets-over-offending-tweet-idUSKCN1WL04T/.

12. https://www.reuters.com/article/us-china-basketball-nba/chinese-basketball-body-halts-cooperation-with-houston-rockets-over-offending-tweet-idUSKCN1WL04T/.

13. https://www.nytimes.com/2019/10/06/sports/daryl-morey-rockets-china.html.

14. David Wells, "Celtics' Enes Kanter Takes Stand Against Nike and NBA Over China," *Daily Mail*, October 28, 2021, https://www.dailymail.co.uk/news/article-10133427/Celtics-Enes-Kanter-slams-China-Nike-LeBron-James-Michael-Jordan-Phil-Knight-slave-labor.html.

15. Eric Gomez, "Daryl Morey Was Misinformed on Tweet About Hong Kong," ESPN, October 18, 2019, https://www.espn.com/nba/story/_/id/27847951/daryl-morey-was-misinformed-sending-tweet-china-hong-kong.

16. LeBron James (@KingJames), X post, January 15, 2018, 2:45 p.m., https://twitter.com/KingJames/status/952902403422150657.

17. Enes Freedom (@EnesFreedom), X post, October 15, 2019, 8:30 a.m., https://twitter.com/EnesFreedom/status/1183949336901816326.

18. Scott Polacek, "Celtics' Enes Kanter Joins Protestors in Boston to Chant 'I Can't Breathe,'" Bleacher Report, June 3, 2020, https://bleacherreport.com/articles/2894293-celtics-enes-kanter-chants-i-cant-breathe-with-protestors-in-boston.

19. Tom Goldman, "A Dramatic Day of No Action in Pro Sports," NPR, August 26,

2020, https://www.npr.org/sections/live-updates-protests-for-racial-justice/2020/08/26/906496470/a-dramatic-day-in-pro-sports-where-the-action-was-no-action.

20. Amnesty International, "Amnesty International Report on Forced Labor in Xinjiang," 2021, https://xinjiang.amnesty.org/wp-content/uploads/2021/06/ASA_17_4137-2021_Full_report_ENG.pdf.

21. Ken Moritsugu, "China Compels Uighurs to Work in Nike Supplier Shoe Factory," AP News, February 28, 2020, https://apnews.com/article/ap-top-news-international-news-weekend-reads-china-health-269b3de1af34e17c1941a514f78d764c.

22. https://www.youtube.com/watch?v=uBCk6AJLaKc.

CHAPTER 10: EXILE

1. https://www.washingtonpost.com/world/asia_pacific/china-compels-uighurs-to-work-in-shoe-factory-that-supplies-nike/2020/02/28/ebddf5f4-57b2-11ea-8efd-0f904bdd8057_story.html.

2. Associated Press, "Enes Kanter Slams China's Xi Jinping Over Tibet," CNBC, October 21, 2021, https://www.cnbc.com/2021/10/21/nba-china-boston-celtics-enes-kanter-slams-xi-over-tibet.html.

3. Brian Windhorst, "Chinese Media Pull Boston Celtics Games After Enes Kanter's Free Tibet Comments," ESPN, October 21, 2021, https://www.espn.com.au/nba/story/_/id/32445320/chinese-media-remove-boston-celtics-games-center-enes-kanter-free-tibet-statements.

4. Garry Kasparov's X post, @Kasparov63, October 20, 2021, https://twitter.com/Kasparov63/status/1451016975279435777.

5. Jonathan White, "NBA Star Enes Kanter Slams Xi Jinping over Uygur 'Genocide' in Xinjiang," *South China Morning Post*, October 23, 2021, https://www.scmp.com/sport/basketball/article/3153445/nba-star-enes-kanter-slams-xi-jumping-over-uygur-genocide-xinjiang.

6. Darren Rovell, "NBA Signs 8-Year Deal with Nike," ESPN, June 10, 2015, https://www.espn.com/nba/story/_/id/13053413/nba-signs-8-year-apparel-deal-nike.

NOTES

7. Ben Church, "Enes Kanter Says Nike Is 'Scared to Speak Up' Against China and Wears 'Modern Day Slavery' Shoes in Protest of Uyghur Treatment," CNN, October 26, 2021, https://www.cnn.com/2021/10/26/football/enes-kanter-nike-china-protest-spt-intl/index.html.

8. Robert F. Kennedy Jr. post, X, October 25, 2021, https://x.com/KennedyNation/status/1453152063777562632.

9. Nathan Law post, X, @NathanLawKC, October 25, 2021, https://x.com/nathanlawkc/status/1453082615867707395.

10. Shebnem77 post, X, October 2021, https://x.com/Shebnem77/status/1453750076225081351https://x.com/Shebnem77/status/1453750076225081351.

11. Carlitosonchina post, X, @carlitosonchina, October 2021, https://x.com/carlitosonchina/status/1453155262315917316.

12. https://twitter.com/EnesFreedom/status/1461380967197814785/photo/1.

13. "NBA Players Face Questions about Shoe Deals with Chinese Companies Linked to Forced Labor," ESPN, January 17, 2022, https://www.espn.com/nba/story/_/id/33140405/nba-players-face-questions-shoe-deals-chinese-companies-linked-forced-labor.

14. Ronald Reagan, Remarks at the Presentation Ceremony for the Presidential Medal of Freedom, November 5, 1985, Ronald Reagan Presidential Library, https://www.reaganlibrary.gov/archives/speech/remarks-presentation-ceremony-presidential-medal-freedom-5.

15. David Frum, "Why Enes Kanter Freedom Speaks Out," *Atlantic*, December 8, 2021, https://www.theatlantic.com/ideas/archive/2021/12/why-enes-kanter-freedom-speaks/620940/.

16. Enes Kanter Freedom photo, Instagram, December 2021, https://www.instagram.com/p/CX_lX4BloQA/?igsh=MWk4YXltcXk5NXdlaw%3D%3D.

17. "Boston Celtics Game Broadcast Pulled in China over Enes Kanter's Pro-Tibet Posts," *BBC Sports*, January 2022, https://www.bbc.com/sport/basketball/59987418.

18. Michael Waltz video post, Facebook, January 2022, https://www.facebook.com/MichaelWaltzForCongress/videos/286923340028273/.

19. Ben Church, "Enes Kanter Freedom vs. Yao Ming on NBA and China," CNN, January 19, 2022, https://www.cnn.com/2022/01/19/sport/enes-kanter-freedom-yao-ming-nba-china-spt-intl/index.html.

CHAPTER 12: FREEDOM'S FUTURE

1. Enes Kanter Freedom, Testimony before the Congressional House Committee on Homeland Security, January 17, 2024, U.S. Congress, https://www.congress.gov/118/meeting/house/116737/witnesses/HHRG-118-HM05-Wstate-FreedomE-20240117.pdf.